THE ILLUSTRATED HISTORY OF THE WORLD

Conflict and Change

PREFACE

*T*he *Illustrated History of the World* is a unique series of eight volumes
covering the entire scope of human history, from the days of the nomadic
hunters up to the present. Each volume surveys significant events and
personages, key political and economic developments, and the critical forces
that inspired change, in both institutions and the everyday life of people around
the globe.

The books are organized on a spread-by-spread basis, allowing ease of
access and depth of coverage on a wide range of fascinating topics and time
periods within any one volume. Each spread serves as a kind of mini-essay,
in words and pictures, of its subject. The text—cogent, concise and lively—is
supplemented by an impressive array of illustrations (original art, full-color
photographs, maps, diagrams) and features (glossary, index, time charts,
further reading listings). Taking into account the new emphasis on
multicultural education, special care has been given to presenting a balanced
portrait of world history: the volumes in the series explore all civilizations—
whether it's the Mayans in Mexico, the Shoguns in Japan or the Sumerians in
the Middle East.

Conflict and Change

·

Fiona Reynoldson

Facts On File

Facts On File, Inc.
460 Park Avenue South
New York NY 10016

Library of Congress Cataloging-in-Publication Data

Reynoldson, Fiona
Conflict and change/Fiona Reynoldson.
p.   cm. — (Illustrated history of the world)
Includes bibliographical references and index.
Summary: Explores the history of the world from 1650 to 1800 with
emphasis on the agricultural revolution, the Enlightenment, the
Industrial Revolution, the American and French Revolutions, Manchu
China, and Shogunate Japan.
ISBN 0-8160-2790-0
1. History, Modern—17th century—Juvenile literature.
2. History, Modern—18th century—Juvenile literature.
[1. History, Modern—17th century. 2. History, Modern—18th
century. 3. World History.] I. Title. II. Series: Illustrated
history of the world (New York, N.Y.)
D246.R49 1993
909.7—dc20
92-20460
CIP
AC

ISBN 0 8160 2790 0

Facts On File books are available at special discounts when purchased
in bulk quantities for businesses, associations, institutions or sales
promotions. Please call our Special Sales Department in New York at
212/683-2244 (dial 800/322-8755 except in NY, AK or HI).

Designed by Hammond Hammond
Composition by Goodfellow and Egan Ltd, Cambridge
Printed and Bound by BPCC Hazell Books, Paulton and Aylesbury

10 9 8 7 6 5 4 3 2 1

This book is printed on acid-free paper.

First Published in Great Britain in 1991 by
Simon and Schuster Young Books

CONTENTS

INTRODUCTION

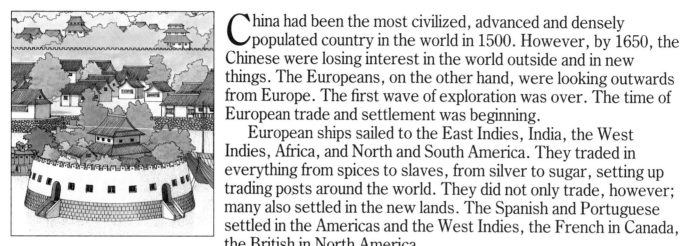

China had been the most civilized, advanced and densely populated country in the world in 1500. However, by 1650, the Chinese were losing interest in the world outside and in new things. The Europeans, on the other hand, were looking outwards from Europe. The first wave of exploration was over. The time of European trade and settlement was beginning.

European ships sailed to the East Indies, India, the West Indies, Africa, and North and South America. They traded in everything from spices to slaves, from silver to sugar, setting up trading posts around the world. They did not only trade, however; many also settled in the new lands. The Spanish and Portuguese settled in the Americas and the West Indies, the French in Canada, the British in North America.

The Europeans were forging ahead in agriculture too. Europe and China were the two main areas of the world where farmers used the plough instead of digging by hand. This meant that more land could be farmed and so more food could be grown.

The *Renaissance* in the fifteenth century had led to a tradition of art, science and thinking that was accepted at all the great courts of Europe. Advances in science led on to advances in industry, agriculture and transport. As far as armies were concerned, guns remained fairly primitive, but changes in organization led to more disciplined, professional armies than there had been before. These armies were used by the powers of Europe to fight firstly for territory in Europe and secondly for new lands overseas.

The effect of the Europeans on the world in the seventeenth and eighteenth centuries was like a stone thrown into a pond, causing ripples that spread out further and further. Europe affected all the world to a greater or lesser extent. Only the very edges of the world were still untouched by 1800.

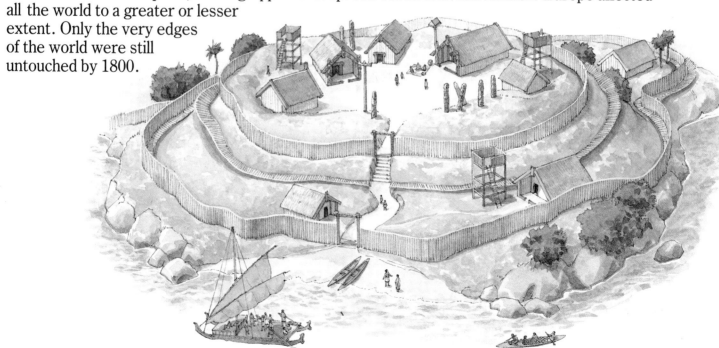

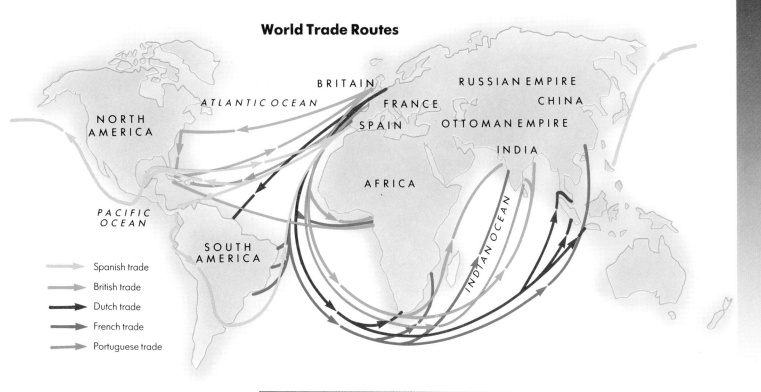

- Spanish trade
- British trade
- Dutch trade
- French trade
- Portuguese trade

Labels on map: BRITAIN, ATLANTIC OCEAN, FRANCE, SPAIN, RUSSIAN EMPIRE, CHINA, OTTOMAN EMPIRE, INDIA, NORTH AMERICA, AFRICA, INDIAN OCEAN, PACIFIC OCEAN, SOUTH AMERICA

PART ONE

Changes in Europe

The European voyages of discovery in the fifteenth and sixteenth centuries were not the first journeys that people had made across the oceans. We know that the *Vikings* had sailed from Europe to America several hundred years earlier. Others had traveled across the Pacific Ocean on rafts from the western coast of South America. New Zealand had been reached by the *Maoris* from Pacific islands by the fourteenth century. The *Aleuts* and the *Inuits* had crossed the Bering Strait from Siberia to North America about 12,000 years ago. There are probably many other sea voyages that people made in the long-distant past about which we have no clues as yet.

However many voyages there may have been, none of them had the instant impact that the European voyages of discovery had in the sixteenth century.

OPENING UP THE WORLD Suddenly the world was opening up as it never had before. By 1650 there were sea routes to the Far East, to Africa and to the Americas, so that all sorts of goods could be brought to Europe. The voyages were risky and often ships were lost at sea, but the risk was worth it for the gains that were made. Trade was no longer confined largely to the

Mediterranean Sea and around the coasts of lands like China, Japan, the East Indies, India and Africa. In 1650, trade was on the edge of becoming global. By 1800, it was global.

At first Spain and Portugal dominated the scene. Then they were challenged by the Netherlands, France and Britain—powerful countries with good ocean ports.

THE WORLD OUTSIDE EUROPE Meanwhile, life went on in the rest of the world as it had for thousands of years. China and India had their own high levels of civilization and culture, stretching back for hundreds of years. Many of the societies which we call "primitive" lived in harmony with nature, as people did not see themselves as separate from nature. There is a story about an Australian Aboriginal who, in trying to explain this, sat beneath a tree and painted a line up his body and then continued to paint the line up the tree. He and the tree were part of the same life and energy of the world.

The Europeans, however, had little respect for any culture that was different to their own. As the search to expand trade and influence turned to colonial settlement, especially after 1800, the Europeans tried to impose their way of life on the peoples they dominated.

EUROPE IN 1650

A group of French Huguenot refugees landing at Dover in southern England in 1685. After the Edict of Nantes was passed as a law in France, Huguenots (Protestants) were not allowed to practice their religion there.

Europe was just emerging from nearly half a century of a war in which there had been huge casualties. Divisions over religion had been a major cause of the persecutions and fighting since the *Reformation* in the early sixteenth century. Catholics and Protestants had fought each other and had claimed that each was in the right and was following the one true religion of Christ. By the middle of the seventeenth century, many religious refugees had been forced to leave their countries and find a home elsewhere.

The *Huguenots*, for instance, were French Protestants who had been persecuted in Catholic France. Many moved to England and to the northern Netherlands. They were great weavers and in both countries they helped to bring about the rise of the cloth industries. Other Protestant refugees went to Switzerland and contributed to the growing craft industries there. The *Pilgrim Fathers* were a group of over 100 men and women who did not feel that England gave them enough freedom to practice their religion. They sailed to North America in 1620 to found a new colony on the east coast.

POPULATION GROWTH The restlessness was not only due to religious persecution. The population of Europe had risen dramatically in the sixteenth century and, by 1650, much of Europe no longer grew enough food to feed its population. This was a very serious situation. Spain had been a great power, but by the seventeenth century it was in decline. Part of the reason for this was that farming did not keep pace with the population. Spain was taking huge amounts of gold and silver from the mines in South America, but people cannot eat gold and silver. Spain had to use this money to buy food, such as wheat from Poland. It was becoming obvious that the gold and silver had not made Spain rich. Instead, these precious metals were passing through the country to pay for all the goods the Spanish needed, but did not grow or make.

CHANGES IN AGRICULTURE The growing population all over Europe was a key factor in everything that happened in the world between 1650 and 1800. For instance, the European explorers had brought the potato back from South America at the end of the sixteenth century and had found it grew well in Europe. If you plant a field with potatoes, you can feed four times the number of people than if you plant the field with wheat. The potato, together with huge imports of wheat from Poland, helped to feed the population of Europe, and encouraged it to grow.

Apart from new foods, new ways of farming to grow more food were also needed. This led to the Agricultural Revolution. The need to make things to sell for money that would buy food was a factor in the coming Industrial Revolution. Iron ore was found in places like Britain, so people there could make machines of iron to sell to other places and then use the money to buy food.

THE URGE TO EXPAND If this was all that was needed, Europe might have remained trading within its own boundaries. But the explorers had already shown that there was a world outside. They had shown that it was possible to sail anywhere. They had shown that marvelous foods, cloth, porcelain and jewels could be brought back to Europe to make life better and more interesting for those Europeans rich enough to pay for them. The prospect was irresistible.

European Expansion 1500–1775

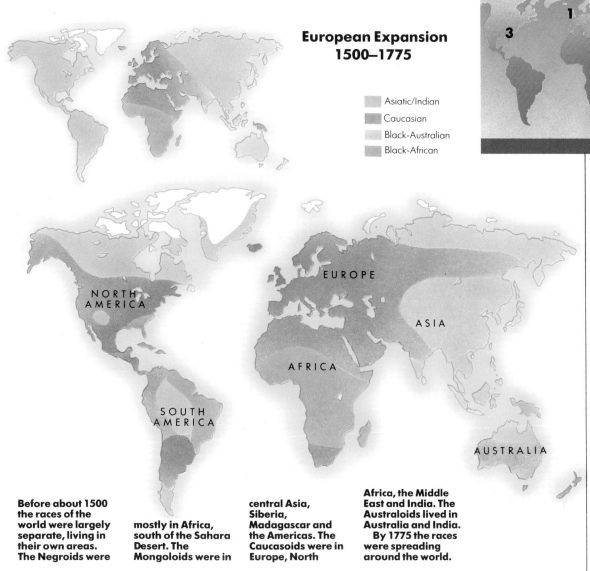

Asiatic/Indian
Caucasian
Black-Australian
Black-African

NORTH AMERICA

EUROPE

ASIA

AFRICA

SOUTH AMERICA

AUSTRALIA

Before about 1500 the races of the world were largely separate, living in their own areas. The Negroids were mostly in Africa, south of the Sahara Desert. The Mongoloids were in central Asia, Siberia, Madagascar and the Americas. The Caucasoids were in Europe, North Africa, the Middle East and India. The Australoids lived in Australia and India.

By 1775 the races were spreading around the world.

1 In 1642 civil war broke out between King Charles I and Parliament in Britain. In 1645, Parliament's New Model Army crushed the king's forces at the Battle of Naseby. Charles escaped to Scotland but was "sold" to Parliament for £400,000. In 1649 he was executed and England was declared a Commonwealth. In 1651 Cromwell, leading the Parliamentary forces, defeated the new king, Charles II, at Worcester. Charles fled to France. In 1660 he was invited back to England to be king again. This was known as the Restoration.

2 In 1669 the Mogul Emperor Aurangzeb banned the Hindu religion and ordered all the non-Islamic schools and temples to be destroyed. Because of this there was more and more unrest in his empire. This led to the break-up of the Mogul Empire in 1707.

3 The Europeans were exploring and settling North America at this time. In 1664 the British gave the name New York to the town then called New Amsterdam. In 1673 French explorers reached the headwaters of the Mississippi River, and eight years later a Frenchman called La Salle explored the whole length of the Mississippi River. In 1683, the first German immigrants settled in America.

World Population Figures

In AD 1 the world's population was about 300 million. By AD 1650 it had reached 600 million and by 1800 it was 1 billion. At first the population level grew slowly—between AD 1000 and 1750 it rose by about one tenth of 1 per cent a year. Many babies were born, but only about half of them lived to the age of five. Famines and epidemics kept the rate of growth very slow.

From AD 1750 the world's population grew rapidly. This

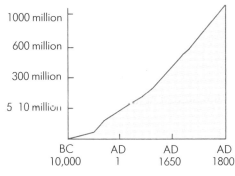

1000 million
600 million
300 million
5 10 million

BC 10,000 — AD 1 — AD 1650 — AD 1800

was particularly so in Europe and North America. The huge rises in population, however, came after 1800.

Not only did numbers rise but the races of the world became more mixed

after 1650. Europeans moved into the Americas and Australia. Africans moved to the Americas. Chinese, Indians and Russians moved to new areas as well.

Eastern Imports

European ships brought back spices from the East, such as nutmeg and pepper, to flavor the dull, bland (and sometimes not very fresh) winter foods of Europe. Fine porcelain came from China, along with silk that was much softer to wear than rough woollen cloth. Jars like this one were so precious that they often had silver rims to prevent chipping.

DIVISIONS OF SOCIETY IN EUROPE

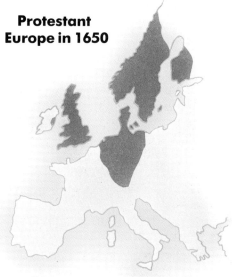

Left. Sir Roger de Coverly, a rich landowner in England, going to church. The people around are tenants farming land on his estates. They are dressed in their best clothes and show great respect to him.

Above. A well-dressed Russian nobleman and a serf.

In 1650, Europe was still in many ways a *feudal* society. Nobles no longer held land from their king or queen in return for raising an army of knights and going to fight for them; instead they now owned their land themselves. But in most other ways the nobles behaved in a feudal way. From Russia to Spain, they expected to be the close advisers of their king or queen. They expected the highest positions in governments and in the army. In some countries, like France, only members of the nobility were allowed the highest jobs. In most countries the nobles lived for most of the year on their estates. Some were good managers, but they all expected their peasants to work their land in a way that seems like slavery to us.

SERFDOM The situation varied across Europe, and there was a general difference between eastern and western Europe. In eastern Europe the *serfs*, who had to work on the land, had become less free. From 1593, in Russia, serfs were no longer allowed the two weeks a year of free movement that they had previously been

Feudalism

Up to the Middle Ages, European nobles had held their land from the king. The king owned all the land of a country (often because he had conquered it in war), but he could not farm it and run it all alone. He would allow his friends and fighting companions to farm and run large areas of land for him. They did not own the land. They held it in return for swearing loyalty to the king and serving him in the army or government. This was called feudalism.

Protestant Europe in 1650

Mostly Protestant

By 1550 nearly 40% of the population of Europe belonged to some sort of Protestant religion. By 1650 this figure had fallen to about 20%. The two largest countries that were won back to Catholicism were France and Poland.

Monarchs, Parliament and Society

Kings and queens, (left), were still very powerful in most of Europe, particularly in France, Prussia, Austria and Russia.

The Catholic and Protestant Churches relied on the monarch and Parliament for support.

In some countries, particularly Britain and the Netherlands, Parliament's power was growing.

Merchants and bankers became more important as trade developed. They usually supported Parliament.

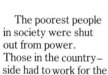

Well-established landowners often supported the monarch, while recent landowners usually did not.

The influential Members of Parliament were lawyers, because they were skilled in discussions.

The army often supported Parliament. During the English Civil War (1642–1649) Cromwell led an army against the king.

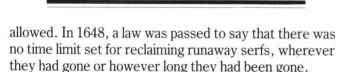

The poorest people in society were shut out from power. Those in the country-side had to work for the landowners, while those in the towns worked for the merchants, bankers, lawyers and so on.

Above. A painting of the inside of a farmhouse by Jan Brueghel (1568–1625). How many people and animals are in the kitchen? How many activities are going on?

Left. Cardinal Richelieu (1585–1642) was a bishop by the time he was 21. At 39 he was the chief minister of the royal household and was virtually the ruler of France. He made the king's government very strong.

allowed. In 1648, a law was passed to say that there was no time limit set for reclaiming runaway serfs, wherever they had gone or however long they had been gone.

In western Europe, serfdom had all but disappeared. This did not mean that peasants working on the land in these countries were better off. In France they were bowed down with taxes. In the German states, a great deal of land had been ruined during the fighting in the Thirty Years' War, which had ended in 1648. However poor the peasants, the nobles made sure they had plenty of money with which to build their houses, hunt and dress well.

THE CLERGY The clergy were another large section of society in seventeenth and eighteenth century Europe. Whether Catholic or Protestant, bishops and lesser clergymen represented the Church in their countries. The clergy were meant to look after the spiritual needs of all the people. In return, the people were expected to pay a tithe (tenth) of their income to support the clergyman who lived locally. This was yet one more

burden on the poor. It was one that became more resented as people began to resent the amount of land the Church owned and the fact that many clergy did not do their jobs very well. In France, cardinals, such as Richelieu in the seventeenth century, were also politicians. In Germany, some bishops lived like princes. In England, by the eighteenth century, some clergymen were going fox-hunting and living the life of idle gentlemen.

THE THIRD ESTATE The nobles and clergy were known during this period as the *First and Second Estates*. The *Third Estate* was the commoners. This included merchants, lawyers, farmers and so on—in fact, everyone who was not noble or in the Church.

These were the divisions that existed in most of Europe in 1650. They were not found in Switzerland or in the new Dutch Republic. Neither of these countries had a king or a nobility. On the whole the ordinary people there—the Third Estate—were much freer to take part in the government of the country.

FARMING THE LAND

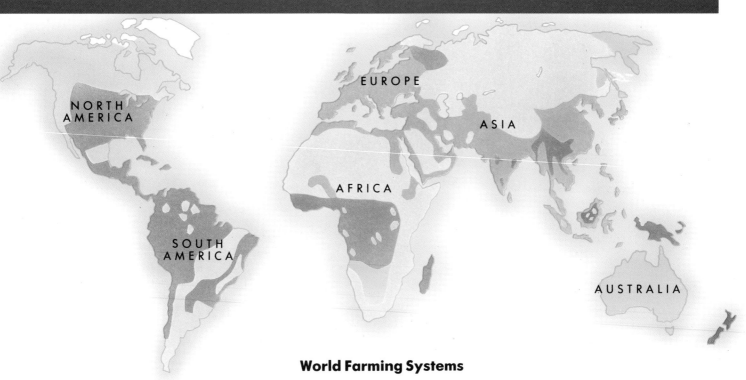

World Farming Systems

farming (using a plough)

herders

farming (digging by hand)

hunter-gatherers

Most people in the world at this time spent their lives looking for or producing their own food, as there was little industry. The map above shows the different types of farming in different parts of the world.

The majority of people in Europe lived off the land. In 1650, over three-quarters of the world's land surface was occupied by *hunter-gatherers* or by *herdsmen*. Only about one-quarter of the land was under the plough. However, ploughing and farming land produced far more food than the other ways of life did. This one-quarter of the world's land surface was probably producing enough food for three-quarters of the world's population.

FARMING AREAS Most of the land being ploughed and farmed was located in an area running from China, through India, to the Middle East and Europe. A small part of Russia and North Africa was also included in this farming land.

Nowadays, in developed countries, we can import food from other countries and we can preserve food by many methods, such as refrigeration. This means that what we eat does not vary a great deal throughout the year. Nor do we worry if crops such as wheat or oranges fail in one area because of bad weather, as we can always buy these foods from another area. However, this was not so in 1650, when most people in the world had to produce their food themselves. In good years there would be a little over to sell to the small numbers of people who lived in towns.

TYPES OF FARM In Europe, most farmers had small areas of land, each averaging between 5 and 25 acres. Sometimes this land was not all in one place, but was scattered in small strips of land around the village. Usually only an orchard or vegetable garden was right next to the farmer's small cottage. Each farmer and family might produce about 20 percent more than they ate, kept for seed for next year or used to make clothes. The rest was sold at local markets.

What crops were grown and what animals were kept depended on the climate. In northwest Europe, wheat, barley, oats, rye, milk, cheese, butter, eggs and timber were important. Further south, some wheat and other grains like barley, millet and sorghum were grown, together with fruits, olives, wine, rice and sugar.

THE YEARLY PATTERN Whatever the crops, the work of all farmers, from Scotland to China, depended on the seasons and the climate. In Europe, in spring, the

Farming in North America

By 1690 farming settlements were scattered along the eastern coast of North America.

At first the settlers brought their tools, animals and seed for growing crops with them from Europe. But they found the land was not very fertile and the seeds that were suitable for the short north European summers did not grow well in North America. They adapted their crops and learned from the native Amerindians to grow crops such as maize, soya beans, pumpkins and sunflowers. These foods were new to the settlers, as they did not grow in Europe.

Below. Tools of the period as shown in an illustrated book.

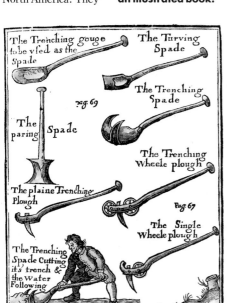

Below. Countrywomen on their way to market.

Farmers' wives traditionally looked after the poultry and cows. Often they took the eggs, hens, butter or cheese to market in the local town and kept the profits they made as their own money.

A countrywoman carrying birds to market. Before the days of refrigerators, many animals were sold live to keep them fresh.

farmers ploughed and sowed seeds and turned their animals out to graze in the fields. In summer, they weeded, cut the hay and tended the animals. Early autumn was the busiest time, because crops had to be harvested. Wheat had to be cut, stacked and stored. In the south, grapes were picked, crushed and made into wine. Fruit was picked and preserved.

Lastly, in the cold north of Europe, winter meant that the grass stopped growing. Therefore, only enough animals were kept through the winter to start breeding from when spring came. Slaughtering and salting down the meat was the last autumn ritual of the harvest. There was a good feast and then, all over north Europe, men and women settled down to a quiet winter, keeping warm and trying to make the food last till spring. The cows that had been saved had to be fed on hay (dried grass). When that ran out, the children gathered holly for them to eat. Sometimes in the spring the cows and sheep were so weak they had to be carried to the fields.

In the vast areas of northern China, a similar yearly routine went on. In hotter lands, the routine varied according to the rainy season rather than the cold.

Everywhere in the farming world, if the crops failed hundreds of thousands of people starved.

1 By 1650 China was still a very powerful and advanced country. Most farming there was on small farms which were worked very hard and which produced high yields. Hardly any dairy goods were produced, because cattle need large areas of land, but there were many pigs and chickens. Improvements in the types of rice grown meant that at least two crops a year could be raised in the south. In the north, where it was colder, wheat had mostly replaced millet and sorghum as a main crop by this time.

2 In India, like China, most farmers grew enough to feed themselves, with some surpluses to use for trade. Rice was grown in the south and wheat in the north. As with China, spices such as pepper and ginger were grown for export. India was also a source of sugar at this time; later, western Europe started to get sugar from plantations in the West Indies and a little from beet grown in Europe.

3 In Australia, the Aboriginals were almost entirely hunter-gatherers, as they had been for thousands of years. Aboriginals near the coast gathered shellfish and fished in the rivers and sea. Further inland they ate a great variety of plants and animals.

THE AGRICULTURAL REVOLUTION

Two main changes took place in farming in Europe between 1650 and 1800. One was that new crops were grown. Most of these came from the Americas and they included maize and potatoes, which began to be widely grown in Europe and even reached as far as China. These new crops meant that more people could be fed.

WAYS OF FARMING The second change, in ways of farming, was called the Agricultural Revolution. Changes made during this period made farming more efficient, so that more food could be grown to feed the increasing population.

The Dutch started *reclaiming land* from lakes and from the sea, using windmills to drive pumps to drain the water away. By 1715, they had reclaimed 368,828 acres. The British used the Dutch methods to drain many square kilometers of land in eastern England, which became rich farmland.

Dutch Land Reclamation

Left. Map showing how the Dutch reclaimed land that was below sea level. They used windmills to pump the water from the low-lying land into canals.

- land reclaimed before 1600
- land reclaimed between 1600 and 1800

NORTH SEA

ZUIDER ZEE

● AMSTERDAM

NETHERLANDS

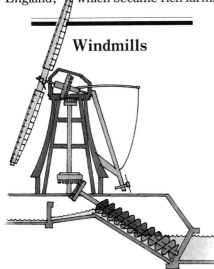

Windmills

A windmill has sails or blades mounted on arms connected to machinery inside. The machinery could be big circular stones to grind corn, or an Archimedes screw (as shown in the picture) for raising water. The Dutch drained the land that lay below sea level in this way. The sails had to face the wind, so the whole windmill (or the top of it, to which the sails were attached) had to be moved around when the wind direction changed. Until 1750 this was done by hand. Then a fantail was invented which helped "blow" it round.

But these methods were expensive in manpower and money, so every centimeter of reclaimed land had to be used. The old way of farming was to leave one field *fallow* (resting) every third year, so that it would not become drained of nourishment. To the land-hungry Dutch this was a waste of land. They worked out a system of *crop rotation*, growing a different type of crop on the same field each year. Each crop took different chemicals and minerals from the soil.

Because of crop rotation, the amount of land that could be farmed increased by one-third—a large jump. However, these methods were slow to spread, although Belgium copied the Dutch, and wealthy farmers in Britain took up the new ideas with enthusiasm.

MACHINERY New machines for cultivating the land were invented in the eighteenth century. One of these was Jethro Tull's seed drill. Previously, three-quarters of the seed might be lost when it was thrown on to the bare field, as the wind blew some away, or some fell on stony ground where it could not grow. The seed drill dug a hole, the seed trickled in and then the hole was covered with earth.

Once seeds were sown in rows it was also easier to weed between them. Another new machine was a horse hoe, which used a horse to pull several hoes, so that several rows of seeds could be weeded at once.

New farming magazines appeared. Farmers read them and learnt about new methods of manuring and caring for their land. Arthur Young wrote in 1768:

Around Bridgend there are many farms which consist of very light land, and yet no turnips are sown. One farmer from England, sowed two acres, and was at great pains to hoe them well; the neighbours ridiculed him and really thought him mad; but were surprised to see what a great crop he gained.

IMPROVEMENTS IN ANIMAL BREEDING Another great improvement was in animal breeding. Robert Bakewell, who was born at Dishley in Leicestershire in 1725, was just one of many pioneers of new methods in this area during the eighteenth century. In 1700, the average British cow weighed about 374 pounds. By breeding the biggest, fattest cows with the biggest, fattest bulls, the weight of the average cow had reached 792 pounds by 1800.

Thus, despite its rising population, Europe could be fed. By 1700, the Netherlands was exporting 90 percent of its cheese. Denmark sent 80,000 cattle a year to Germany. By 1750, about 17 percent of Britain's exports were food. The changes in farming in northwest Europe were paying off.

the first year wheat might be grown; the second year, clover; the third year, barley; and the fourth year, turnips. Each crop took different chemicals from the soil. Some crops like legumes (peas, beans, etc.) put nitrates back into the soil.

Left. Jethro Tull's seed drill. Notice the hoppers (boxes) that held the seed. Rakes covered the seed and also sowed it in rows, making it easier to weed between crops. Crop rotation meant sowing a different crop in a field each year. In

Above right. A Lincolnshire bull painted by George Stubbs. Many rich farmers at this time commissioned artists to paint their prize animals. The artists always painted them as large and fat as possible to please their owners.

Key Dates for Agricultural Developments

end 1600s	Four-course rotation established in Norfolk
	Drainage of fens in England
	Enclosure of farmland in Germany
early 1700s	Rotherham plough (like modern plough) first used in Netherlands and Britain
1730s	Jethro Tull invents seed drill and horse hoe in Britain
1760–1820	Peak time of enclosure of open land in England
1770–1790	First machines introduced for chopping turnips, winnowing and threshing
1783	First factory to make ploughs set up in England

TOWN LIFE IN THE SEVENTEENTH CENTURY

Because the population of the world rose in the sixteenth century, more and more people lived in towns. The Chinese had long had a flourishing town life, with cities of over a million people. By 1650, cities in Europe were beginning to grow large too.

DISEASE One problem with large towns was disease, because people lived close together. There were always diseases like typhoid and others caught from dirty water supplies. For instance, in London, all the sewage ran out into rivers such as the Fleet and the Tyburn, which then joined up with the River Thames. Many Londoners went to the Thames for their drinking water and could catch diseases from the sewage in it.

Another disease that ravaged Europe for several hundred years was the *plague*, which last appeared in Britain in 1665. The Bill of Mortality for London in that year lists 68,596 dead of the plague. The usual death toll was about 25,000 a year.

THE GREAT FIRE Fire was another large problem in towns. In 1666 came the Great Fire of London. After a long, dry summer, a baker's oven caught light one night in September and a strong wind soon had the fire raging through the city. The streets were narrow and the buildings were made of wood. In a few days over half the city of London, including St. Paul's Cathedral, was burnt to the ground. People searched among the ashes for lost belongings, a fortnight after the fire had gone out, the cinders still burned the soles of their shoes. Medieval and Tudor London had gone.

THE NEW LONDON The new city was to be built of brick and stone. Many people made grand plans for wide, straight roads, but in the end people clung to the plots of land they owned, so the new houses occupied the same spaces as the old. This meant the streets of London were as narrow as ever.

PARIS London was not the only European city to suffer plague, fires and population growth. Paris, with a population of 400,000, was the largest city in Europe in the seventeenth century, partly because successive kings encouraged rebuilding. For instance, the wooden bridges of Paris were rebuilt in stone. The kings leased plots of land to individuals on condition that the person built according to an agreed plan.

Above. A painting of the Great Fire of London in 1666. The old St. Paul's Cathedral is in the center.

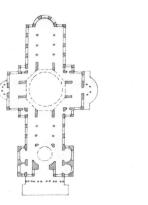

In this way they tried to plan the way in which Paris grew. There were new designs available for houses.

A TOWN HOUSE A town house might be four stories high. A rich husband and wife each had a separate set of rooms, consisting of a reception room and a bedroom. One or two small rooms, called closets, opened out from the bedroom. These could be dressing rooms, studies or primitive lavatories. Separate bathrooms were rare before 1670. A large tub-like bath would be brought into the bedroom and placed before the fire. Then hot water was carried up the stairs by servants to fill the bath.

Other rooms in the house included a kitchen, dining room and general reception rooms. The senior servants and children slept on the top floors, while the lesser servants slept in the attics, or over the stables which were attached to the house.

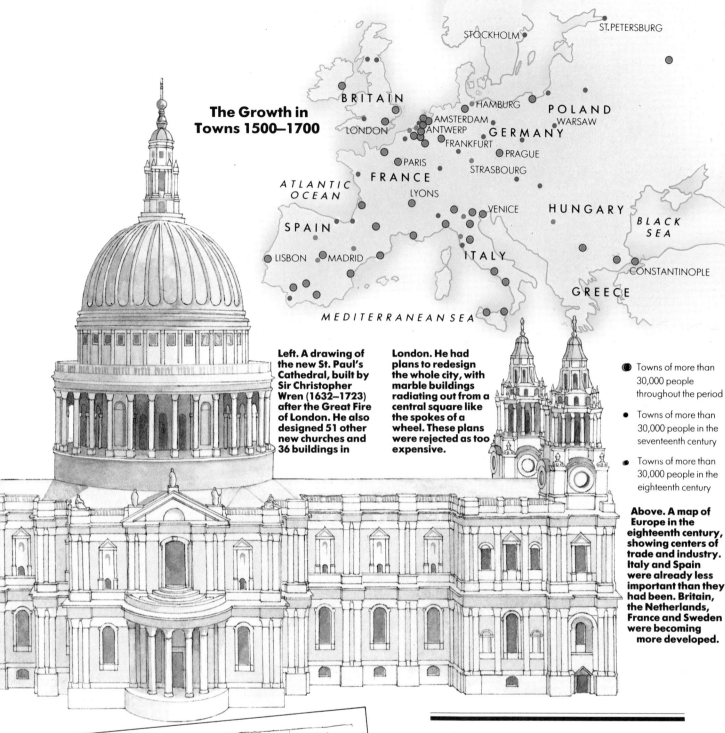

The Growth in Towns 1500–1700

STOCKHOLM · ST. PETERSBURG
BRITAIN
HAMBURG · POLAND
AMSTERDAM · WARSAW
LONDON · ANTWERP · GERMANY
FRANKFURT
PRAGUE
PARIS · STRASBOURG
FRANCE
LYONS
ATLANTIC OCEAN
HUNGARY
VENICE · BLACK SEA
SPAIN
LISBON · MADRID · ITALY
CONSTANTINOPLE
GREECE
MEDITERRANEAN SEA

Left. A drawing of the new St. Paul's Cathedral, built by Sir Christopher Wren (1632–1723) after the Great Fire of London. He also designed 51 other new churches and 36 buildings in

London. He had plans to redesign the whole city, with marble buildings radiating out from a central square like the spokes of a wheel. These plans were rejected as too expensive.

- ● Towns of more than 30,000 people throughout the period
- · Towns of more than 30,000 people in the seventeenth century
- ◑ Towns of more than 30,000 people in the eighteenth century

Above. A map of Europe in the eighteenth century, showing centers of trade and industry. Italy and Spain were already less important than they had been. Britain, the Netherlands, France and Sweden were becoming more developed.

Left. The Bill of Mortality for London in 1665. What did most people die of?

Deadly Diseases

People in Europe, Asia and Africa had had contact with each other for thousands of years. The populations had developed some immunity to the many different diseases that spread from one area to another, even in densely populated towns. However, people in America, Australia and the Pacific Islands had not met the Old World illnesses.

The Amerindian population of Mexico may have been about 30 million before the European conquest in the mid-sixteenth century. Within 100 years it was 3 million. Nine out of every 10 Amerindians had died. Many were deliberately killed, but many more died of Old World diseases such as smallpox, measles, bubonic plague, influenza, tuberculosis, malaria and yellow fever.

19

TOWN LIFE IN THE EIGHTEENTH CENTURY

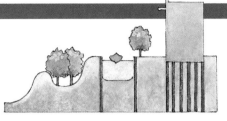

Below. The main thoroughfares in Amsterdam were canals. There were roads lined by trees on both sides of each canal. The gables at the top of the houses were very elaborate. A person could change the style of a house by rebuilding its gables to keep up with the fashion.

Left. Amsterdam was built on peaty soil. This ground had supported the wooden houses of the Middle Ages. However, the Dutch in the seventeenth century wanted to build stone houses that lasted longer. They had to be supported by piles driven down about 10 meters to reach firm, sandy sub-soil.

By the eighteenth century the nobles were not the only people who could afford town houses. Increasingly, merchants who were making money from the growing world trade could also afford fine houses in the towns.

AMSTERDAM One of the greatest centers of this trade was Amsterdam. The Dutch were quite a new nation, who had broken away from Spain in 1579 to become an independent Protestant country, although Spain did not recognize their independence till 1648. Because their land had few natural resources, the Dutch had relied on trade for their livelihood for a long time. They were hardworking and ingenious, and were excellent ship-builders and merchants. By 1700, they were the richest people in Europe. Merchants of the Dutch East India Company imported such luxuries as silk, porcelain, tea, spices and sunshades from the Far East.

HOUSES IN AMSTERDAM The rich Dutch merchants wanted good brick or stone houses like the rich

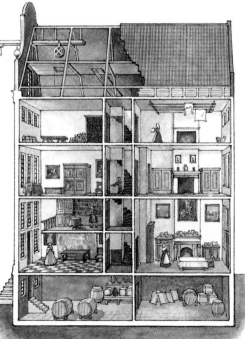

Left. The inside of a Dutch merchant's house. Goods could be stored in the cellar or winched up to the roof. In this house logs and peat for fires are stored in one top room and the laundry is done in the other. (Other families might have used the rooms as extra bedrooms.) Below is a reception room and a bedroom. On the bottom floor is the kitchen with a peat fire. The high-ceilinged room next to it was often the merchant's office. This one has been split into lower and upper rooms.

Above. An engraving by William Hogarth (1697–1764). He specialized in pictures which tell a story. This one is called "Gin Lane." It tells of the horrors of gin-drinking. Gin shops advertised that you could be "Drunk for a penny, dead drunk for two pence; straw to lie in, free." Gin-drinking caused most problems in London between about 1700 and 1750. Then the government put a tax on it and the greater expense meant less gin was drunk. What signs in the picture show that Hogarth thought gin-drinking was dangerous?

Dress Styles

The dresses of rich women were made of silk and lace. For most of this period they were worn over hoops of various widths and shapes.

Wigs were very popular for both men and women. There were many different sorts—full-bottomed wigs, bagwigs, Ramillies wigs (with a long plait and black ribbons), bob wigs and tall, elaborate, individually styled wigs for women. These styles could be very complicated and were sometimes kept in place for weeks, causing itching scalps.

Wig powder was first used in 1703 and white was the most fashionable color. At the height of the powdered wig fashion (1760–1776), blue, violet and dove-pink powders were also used.

everywhere in Europe, but there was a problem. Amsterdam is built on a peaty marsh. The medieval wooden houses were light, while the new brick houses had to be built on piles driven 10 meters deep, down to the hard sub-soil. The foundations were often as expensive as the house, but the Dutch were not put off by this. They built rows of tall, brick houses along the canals, which were the roads of Amsterdam.

Often the front room of the town house was a shop or office. The merchant stored goods in the cellar, or had them winched up to the attic (which was drier). Dutch housewives were very house-proud. The mistress of the house usually did the housework and shopping herself, with the help of a maid. There were fewer servants in the Netherlands than anywhere else in Europe.

VENICE The other city of Europe that was built around a network of canals was Venice. Although it had once been a powerful trading center, by the eighteenth century Venice was a beautiful but declining city. Stuck in a corner of the Mediterranean, it was not in a good position to capture the new trade with the Americas, Africa and the Far East.

LONDON Because it was in an ideal position for trading, London grew rich in the eighteenth century as Britain's trading trebled between 1700 and 1775. People made fortunes in such trades as sugar and tea, and merchants used their wealth to build fine town houses on new land outside the old city of London.

ENTERTAINMENTS In France, the German states and Italy, the nobles dominated the social scene. In Britain, rich merchants and nobles mixed together more often.

The rich enjoyed dancing, music and gambling. There were a number of gentlemen's clubs where you could gamble as much as 50 guineas on each throw of the dice. (A guinea was £1.05.) Balls and assemblies were popular for dancing, and rich parents used these opportunities to choose husbands for their daughters. London and Bath were full of rich young ladies during the Season (April to July) known as the *Marriage Market*.

Absolute Rulers and Empires
THE ABSOLUTE MONARCHS OF FRANCE AND PRUSSIA

The Growth of Prussia

The map above shows the way in which Prussia grew between 1648 (when it became independent of the Holy Roman **Empire) and 1772. Land was taken from Austria, Sweden and Poland. At one time the country included cities as far** **apart as Berlin, Warsaw and Danzig. This growth alarmed other European states.**

VERSAILLES Louis not only worked hard, he wanted to be the most magnificent and powerful king ever. To this end, he built a huge palace at Versailles, 19 miles west of Paris, to house his court, nobles and government. The king became known as the *Sun King* because of the brilliance of his court.

FOREIGN AFFAIRS Louis XIV's aim in foreign affairs was to increase French power, and following this policy meant that from 1667 until 1713 he was almost constantly at war with other European powers. When he was 64 years old, he declared war on Spain, trying to win the Spanish throne for his grandson, Philip. The War of the Spanish Succession lasted for 11 years and bankrupted France. Despite the constant fighting, Louis gained nothing for France.

By 1650, Europe was a continent of emerging *nation-states*. Each one was competing for power and land. During this period a series of *absolute rulers* appeared in many European states. Absolute rulers were those who held all the power for themselves, instead of sharing it with other groups within the state, such as the nobility.

LOUIS XIV (1643–1715) The first and greatest example of an absolute ruler was Louis XIV of France.

Louis inherited the throne of France when he was five years old. Throughout his childhood, there were continual arguments between his mother, who ruled on his behalf, and the council of nobles, who wanted a share of power. When Louis was old enough, therefore, he disbanded the council and said that he would be the only power in the land. He used the words: *L'état c'est moi* ("I am the state").

The young king chose his own advisers and met them every morning to decide everything that should be done, working 12 hours a day for the rest of his long reign.

FREDERICK THE GREAT (1740–1786) Frederick II of Prussia was another great absolute king. He, too, worked long hours and he called himself "the first servant of the state".

Like Louis, he embarked on a number of wars to gain land and power for Prussia. When the Austrian Emperor Charles VI died in 1740, Frederick immediately invaded and conquered Silesia, the part of the Austrian Empire nearest to Prussia. Determined to keep it, he attacked the new empress, Maria Theresa. He had inherited a very efficient and well-organized army from his father and, leading his own troops into battle, he very soon forced Maria Theresa to agree that he could keep the land.

In the years that followed, Frederick was often fighting. Sometimes he was successful, sometimes his armies were cut to pieces, and at one time Berlin itself (the capital of Prussia) was occupied by enemy troops.

His power was absolute within Prussia but, unlike Louis, Frederick did have the interests of his people at

Left. The first stage of Louis XIV's building at Versailles. The architect was Le Vau and the garden designer was Le Notre. In 1678, Louis spent a quarter of the French budget enlarging the new palace. He built two wings, each one the size of the original palace.

Education and Improvements

As with many absolute rulers at this time, Frederick II only wanted better education for the middle classes who would be useful in the civil service. He supported the founding of new schools and a new school-leaving examination, called the *Abitur*, that boys had to pass before going to university. (Girls were not expected to be educated.)

He encouraged new farming methods. He bred cows, sheep and horses and lent the best male animals to landowners so that they could improve their own stock. He supported the enclosing of the big, open fields and the use of fertilizer

heart. For instance, he encouraged agriculture, having the Oberbruch marshes drained and turned into farmland. He also abolished torture and the *censorship* of newspapers.

Frederick encouraged science and education and made the government of Prussia very efficient. When he died, at the age of 74 years, he left behind a strong country and one that was about twice the size that it had been when he came to the throne.

DIFFERENCES BETWEEN FREDERICK AND LOUIS

Frederick II doubled the size of his country, kept Prussia free from debts and was tolerant in religion. The great French thinker, Voltaire, corresponded with Frederick and addressed him as "Your Humanity." Louis XIV, on the other hand, was famous for banning all religions, except Roman Catholicism, and for closing all their churches. He left huge debts and did not succeed in greatly enlarging France.

PETER THE GREAT AND RUSSIA

Peter the Great and the Serfs

Under Peter the Great the serfs became even less free. He brought in a new tax called the "soul tax," to be paid by every male peasant of working age. Each local lord was responsible for collecting the tax from his own serfs. A serf could be moved, sold or exchanged by his master.

Catherine the Great wanted to change this. But she could not, because it was so much a part of the way that farming and the economy were run. The only hope for a badly treated serf was to run away to the borders of the Russian Empire, where it was so wild that he might not be found.

Leeuwenhoek in Holland. His greatest passion was for ships and he even worked (in disguise) as an ordinary shipwright in the Dutch East India Company's shipyards in Amsterdam, humping timber and sawing wood. He took trips on every sort of ship he could, from warships to whalers.

After his return to Russia to put down a rebellion, Peter set about bringing Russian ship-building and industry up to European standards. However, his admirers in Europe were alarmed to hear how he had supervised the torture and execution of leaders of the rebellion. In this his attitude was a long way from that of Frederick II of Prussia (see p. 22).

Although Russia bordered on to Europe, it remained very isolated. One of the reasons for this was that Russia was cut off from trading with Europe, or with anywhere else. For most of the year, its northern sea border was ice-bound. Sweden and Poland blocked the western border. The Turks blocked the southern border. To the east lay deserts and mountains and then China, which was not keen to trade abroad.

PETER THE GREAT (1696–1725) From 1639 on, Russia expanded rapidly (see map). Peter the Great, who became tsar in 1696 at the age of 24, went on a tour of Europe in 1697–98 and saw that Russia was lagging behind. Peter did not just visit kings, he also met scientists like Sir Isaac Newton in England and

IMPROVING RUSSIA In the next 25 years, Peter turned the Russian army, which had been defeated by Sweden, Poland and Turkey, into an up-to-date force. He led it to victory over Sweden in 1721 and gained the provinces of Estonia and Livonia, including a port in the west (called Riga) that was not ice-bound for most of the year.

Peter also built up the Russian navy and made the iron industry as good as any in Europe. He saw clearly, as Frederick the Great did, that he had to make his country more wealthy by improving its farming and

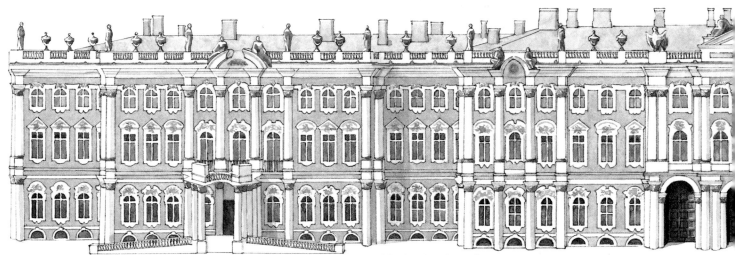

The Winter Palace in St. Petersburg was built by Peter the Great and enlarged for his daughter, the Empress Elizabeth (1741–1762).

The Growth of Russia

ARCTIC OCEAN

ST PETERSBURG

MOSCOW

SIBERIA

NOVGOROD TERRITORY

CASPIAN SEA

ARAL SEA

PACIFIC OCEAN

CHINA

Map showing the growth of Russia in the seventeenth and eighteenth centuries. Trade was one reason for Russia wanting to expand. Russia needed to have overland and sea routes to Europe so that it could trade. Thus Peter the Great fought Sweden for the states on the Baltic Sea and Catherine the Great fought the Turks for land by the Black Sea. In the east, Russia gained more and more land until it reached the Pacific Ocean.

- Territory added 1581–1618
- Territory added 1618–1689
- Territory added in 1650s but returned to China in 1689
- Territory added 1689–1725
- Territory added 1725–1762
- Territory added 1762–1800
- Kazakh territory subject to Russian Empire

industries. Only in this way could Russia become a great power.

THE PEOPLE OF RUSSIA
Unlike Frederick, Peter was not interested in the welfare of his people. The Russian peasants were *serfs*, practically slaves, and remained so until 1861. They worked for Russian nobles who had almost life and death powers over them.

ST. PETERSBURG
Like Louis XIV of France (see p. 22), Peter the Great wanted a grand center of government to reflect his power, so he built the city of St. Petersburg at the mouth of the Neva River. So many people died in making the foundations that it is said to be built on bones.

Catherine the Great married the Grand Duke Peter when she was 16. He became tsar in 1762, but his behaviour was so bad that he was murdered and Catherine became empress.

CATHERINE THE GREAT (1762–1796)
Catherine II, known as Catherine the Great, continued the work of Tsar Peter. She gained land by the Black Sea that included the port of Odessa, giving Russia a port in the south for trading with southern Europe.

At home, Catherine favored better treatment for serfs, but the Russian nobles were too powerful for her to act. Unlike Louis XIV of France, she could not break their power and many Russians continued to be treated as slaves.

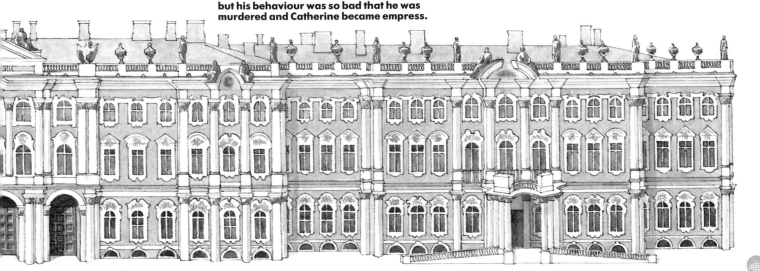

THE WEAKNESS OF TURKEY AND POLAND IN EUROPE

The Decrease of the Ottoman Empire

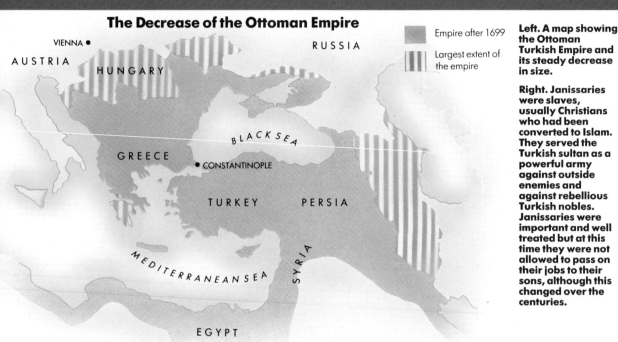

AUSTRIA
VIENNA ●
HUNGARY
RUSSIA
GREECE
BLACK SEA
● CONSTANTINOPLE
TURKEY
PERSIA
MEDITERRANEAN SEA
SYRIA
EGYPT

Empire after 1699

Largest extent of the empire

Left. A map showing the Ottoman Turkish Empire and its steady decrease in size.

Right. Janissaries were slaves, usually Christians who had been converted to Islam. They served the Turkish sultan as a powerful army against outside enemies and against rebellious Turkish nobles. Janissaries were important and well treated but at this time they were not allowed to pass on their jobs to their sons, although this changed over the centuries.

The Turkish Ottoman Empire had been a great and powerful empire under Suleiman the Magnificent (1520–1566). However, by the seventeenth century the empire was being weakened by problems within its various territories, while it was also being challenged from outside by the countries surrounding it.

WEAKNESS OF THE TURKISH EMPIRE After the reign of Suleiman the Magnificent there were a number of weak (and one or two near idiotic) sultans. Added to this, the empire had been built on war. Its elite soldiers were the *janissaries*, who were brought up to be fighting men and became restless if there was no war. By the seventeenth century Turkey was unable to gain any

Right. Sultan Mehmet IV (1648–1687) was more interested in hunting than in running the government.

more land, for the countries around it were too strong, and this prospect of a peaceful, stable empire did not suit the janissaries. They were also discontented because they were badly paid, as Turkey was suffering from rising prices, or *inflation*, so that their wages could not be increased. The silver that flooded in from the Americas in the sixteenth and seventeenth centuries caused inflation all over Europe, and the increasingly weak Turkish Empire was badly affected. To make this problem worse, everyone in the empire had to pay more and more taxes, because all the wars against Persia (Iraq) and Austria in the late sixteenth century had cost the sultan so much money.

THE SIEGE OF VIENNA (1683) Because the Ottoman Empire was a warlike society, one way to prevent rebellions among the soldiers was to send them off to fight a war.

The painting above shows the raising of the siege of Vienna by German and Polish armies on September 12, 1683.

Mehmet IV, who had become sultan in 1648, decided to occupy his army, please people in the empire with a victory and perhaps gain some land by attacking Vienna in Austria. Vienna was only 90 miles from the Turkish frontiers in Europe. Mehmet thought that even if the Turkish army could not hold the city, the army could plunder it and bring the goods home.

The Austrians held out against the Turkish siege for some weeks. Then help came in the form of an army of Germans and Poles led by John Sobieski, the king of Poland (1674–1696). The Turks, who were tired from weeks of besieging Vienna, were outnumbered and defeated and so went home.

This defeat in Austria marked a turning point for Turkey in Europe. Over the course of the next 100 years, Turkey lost a great deal more land to both Austria and Russia.

POLAND Turkey was not the only loser. In the seventeenth century Poland came under attack from Sweden on one of its borders, from the increasingly powerful Russia on the other, and also from Prussia.

Russian armies were based in Poland and Russian ships used Polish ports without permission. Catherine II of Russia (see p. 25) made sure she had the king she wanted on the Polish throne. Finally, at the end of the eighteenth century, Poland's territory was divided

The Partitions of Poland

Left. The growth of Russia on one side, Prussia on another and Austria in the south threatened Poland. Although it fought to stay independent, battles against Sweden finally weakened Poland. Russia, Austria and Prussia took its land.

- Russian, Prussian, Austrian acquisitions in the first partition, 1772
- Russian, Prussian, Austrian acquisitions in the second partition, 1793
- Russian, Prussian, Austrian acquisitions in the third partition, 1795

between Prussia, Russia and Austria.

TURKEY AND RUSSIA Alarmed by the growing Russian strength, the Turks attacked Russia in 1768. But Turkey had been left behind in developments in warfare, so the well-equipped Russians marched into the Turkish Empire and their navy destroyed the Turkish fleet in the Mediterranean. It looked as if the Turkish Empire might collapse altogether.

Industry, Science and the Arts

THE FRENCH COURT AND THE ARTS IN EUROPE

The picture on the left shows a concert at the court of the prince-bishop of Liège (in present-day Belgium). Musical instruments at this time were often highly decorated. The harpsichord, shown above, was a forerunner of the piano. The baryton, pictured on the left, was played with a bow, like a cello, but its strings could also be plucked by the musician's fingers.

The rich nobles of France in the seventeenth and eighteenth centuries led the most luxurious, civilized and glamorous lives of anyone in Europe at that time. They were not allowed to work in trade or industry; instead, they lived on the rent from all the land they owned, and did not have to pay taxes.

Louis XIV built the palace of Versailles (see p.22) to house his court, nobles and government. Anyone who was anyone had to be seen at Versailles. The nobles drove there from Paris in their carriages and the huge gilded halls wcre filled with beautifully dressed people. Louis encouraged his nobles to spend extravagantly, so that they would not have enough money or time to plot rebellions.

The court became a center for musicians and for artists, so it was always crowded. Louis loved dancing—ballet as we know it started at this time. The whole court used to take part in the ballets (not very strenuously) and the king often took the leading parts.

LOUIS XV (1715–1774) Louis XIV's grandson, Louis XV, who came to the throne in 1715 at the age of five, grew up to be quite different. He was a shy man. He kept up the ceremonies such as the *levée* and the *couchée* (the daily public ceremonies of the king rising and of going to bed at night), but when the last noble courtier had gone, Louis got out of bed, put on his dressing-gown and returned to his private rooms for supper and a game of cards with close friends.

THE SALONS Fashionable Parisians copied this more relaxed way of living. Entertaining in salons was usually presided over by the lady of the house and consisted of conversation and the exchange of ideas. One of the most

M ozart could play the harpsichord when he was three, and before he was five he was composing music. At the age of six he was giving concerts all over Europe. He grew up playing the piano and violin, conducting at concerts, teaching the harpsichord and piano, and writing music and operas for money.

When Mozart was 31 his father died, leaving him heavily in debt. He was under great stress, constantly overworked, and suffered from ill-health. He died in 1791 at the age of 35.

Despite his early death, Mozart's life was not a waste, as he wrote over 500 pieces of music as well as his 12 complete operas. These include *The Marriage of Figaro*, *Don Giovanni* and *The Magic Flute*. For many music lovers, he is the finest classical composer who ever lived.

Above. The most famous room in the Palace of Versailles is the Galerie de Glaces (Hall of Mirrors). It was designed by Hardouin-Mansart. The size, and the lavish use of marble, painted ceilings and mirrors, all give the room an overwhelming grandeur.

Eastern Influences

A s the Europeans explored other parts of the world, so they brought back artistic ideas. French settees in this period had legs carved like Egyptian sphinxes.

Wealthy British and French people bought Persian and Indian rugs. The patterns on Chinese porcelain and wallpaper influenced the designs on European tableware and on walls. Cabinets and screens were made of Far Eastern lacquerware.

famous of these hostesses was Madame de Staël, who lived in the late eighteenth century. Some *salons* were very intellectual. Nobles like the Duc de Choiseul mixed with *philosophers*, scientists and writers such as Voltaire, Montesquieu and Rousseau. These gatherings fostered the spirit of free-thinking and enquiry and led to criticism of religion and absolute monarchs. This was one factor that led to the French Revolution (see pp. 50–51).

MUSIC Singing was a favorite entertainment for many people, although only the rich of Europe went to the opera. Italy led the field with comic and serious operas. Other forms of music were popular too. Powerful princes kept their own orchestras. Joseph Haydn was *Kapellmeister* (chief musician) to Prince Esterhazy in Hungary. He produced operas, masses and other music which was listened to by everyone who came to the prince's court. Haydn's music was liked so much that he was showered with invitations to perform all over Europe.

The Austrian composer Mozart worked in a more free-lance way, playing, conducting and composing all over Europe until he died at the age of 35 in 1791. He was not the only musician to travel; for instance, although Handel came from Germany he composed music in England for theaters and for public ceremonies. There were many opportunities to earn a living if you were a gifted musician.

PAINTING Other forms of art also flourished in this period. Styles of painting varied from the Italian Antonio Canaletto, who painted several grand pictures of Venice and London, to the homely paintings of the Dutch artist Jan Vermeer.

THE ENLIGHTENMENT

In the medieval and early modern times, people had been ruled by beliefs in God and also by superstition, but by 1650 there was a new system of ideas. It was called *Reason*. This did not mean that religion or superstition died out; instead people, led by the great scientists and *philosophers*, began more and more to look for reasons *why* things happened. This search for reason and order in the universe grew out of the explorations which had opened up the world. For instance, no one could believe that the world was flat any more. What else might be untrue? A whole new way of looking at this large, spherical planet of ours, and at humankind's place on it, had to be found.

VOLTAIRE AND ROUSSEAU Different thinkers approached the problem of making sense of the world in different ways. The French philosopher, François-Marie Voltaire (1694–1778), criticized the Church and the governments of the time, saying that they were superstitious and did not allow people to think for themselves. He believed that people had a right to think in whichever way they liked, as long as they did not force their ideas on to others. Voltaire is famous for saying: *I disapprove of what you say, but I will defend to the death your right to say it.*

Jean-Jacques Rousseau (1712–1778) wrote plays, operas and articles in encyclopedias. He became interested in so-called "primitive" people and began to wonder if the civilization he lived in was such a good idea. His most famous book, called *The Social Contract*, begins: *People are born free but are everywhere in chains.* Rousseau goes on to say that human beings will win freedom and happiness only if they re-learn the ways of the *"noble savage,"* because "primitive" people are not greedy. They do not try to get more possessions or power than they need.

KANT Immanuel Kant (1724–1804) was a great German thinker who was influenced by the writings of Rousseau and Sir Isaac Newton (see pp. 32–33). As Newton looked for order and laws that governed the way the universe worked, so Kant looked for laws that governed the way human beings lived. He believed that the special ability of human beings was to think and reason. He wrote many books and is famous for his golden rule for living a good life—people should behave as though every action they take will, in future, be made a general rule for everyone to obey.

THE REASON FOR REASON All the great philosophers thought that everything in the world could be done better if there was order and reason. This led to a desire for justice, because in a well-run world there should not be suffering and unfairness. These ideas reached a peak in the American Declaration of Independence (see p. 48) and in the French Revolution (see pp. 50–51).

In this way the ideas of the Enlightenment influenced the lives of ordinary people all over the world, although it took some time for many of the changes to happen.

In a completely different way, the desire for order and reason, together with the rise of scientific thinking, shaped the way that medicine came to be practiced in the Western world, and that affected everybody and made them healthier and longer lived.

The first lecture at Madame Geoffrin's salon in Paris in 1750. Rousseau and Diderot are in the audience.

Mary Wollstonecraft

Left. Voltaire made his name writing plays. He wrote a book called *Letters on the English*, comparing British freedom with French lack of freedom. Because of this he was forced to flee to Switzerland.

Above. Immanuel Kant was interested in mathematics and politics as well as philosophy. His best-known book is the *Critique of Pure Reason*, where he argues that only ideas are real.

Wollstonecraft was a teacher, writer, publisher and translator. She believed that girls should be as well educated as boys. She also wanted to make life better for ordinary people and took a great interest in the French Revolution. When people attacked the revolutionaries, saying that it was against God's laws to rebel against their king, Wollstonecraft wrote a book in reply called *Vindication of the Rights of Man*. She asked what else the revolutionaries could do when the rich people treated them so badly. Many people read her book.

Wollstonecraft's next book, called *Vindication of the Rights of Women*, claimed that women were equal to men.

Left. Jean-Jacques Rousseau began his career writing plays, operas and encyclopedia articles. His work led him to find out about so-called "primitive" peoples. From this he moved on to think about the ways in which people are ruled.

Dr. Samuel Johnson (1709—84)

Below. Denis Diderot (1713–1784) was chief editor of the *Encyclopédie* (left), one of the most important books of the Enlightenment. The aim of the *Encyclopédie* was to further all branches of knowledge, from furniture-making to mathematics.

Pl. 1

Architecture, Carreleur

Johnson was probably the most famous writer in England in the eighteenth century. He is well known today for his *Complete Dictionary of the English Language*, which was supposed to contain every word used in England at the time it was written, together with its correct spelling and meaning.

It took Johnson and his eight assistants seven years to complete the dictionary. It was the first one of its kind, for all other dictionaries had previously only included words that were hard to spell, not every word in the language. Johnson's dictionary included 43,500 words.

THE RISE OF SCIENTIFIC THINKING

The period 1650 to 1800 was a time of great scientific advances. In the Middle Ages learning had been in the hands of the Church. This had often prevented any sort of study that might go against the teaching of the Catholic Church. With the European *Renaissance* of the fifteenth and sixteenth centuries, people began to look at different areas of learning. Men and women were interested in finding out what the great ancient civilizations of Greece and Rome had written about the way in which the world worked. From this they went on to study the world we live in and to try to find out more about it. The *Reformation* in sixteenth-century Europe carried on the work of the Renaissance in breaking the power of the Church as the only authority over people's beliefs and thoughts. By the seventeenth century people were freer to explore all sorts of new ways of looking at things.

SIR ISAAC NEWTON (1642–1727)
One of the greatest scientific thinkers of the seventeenth century was Sir Isaac Newton. When he was young he read the work of the French mathematician René Descartes (1596–1650). He could not agree with what Descartes wrote about light, so he decided to do some experiments himself.

Like Descartes and others, he used a glass object called a *prism* to break up a beam of light into a *spectrum* (the seven colors of the rainbow). He then went further than Descartes by placing another prism, upside down, behind the first one, to make the beams of colored light form back into one beam of white light again. In this way Newton proved that white light is really made up of the colors of the rainbow.

Newton went on to work on telescopes, to produce the theory of gravity and to dabble in *alchemy* in his search for an understanding of the meaning of the world.

Newton's discoveries were the basis of all later scientific thinking and no scientist or thinker has been untouched by them. But he knew he was only at the beginning of understanding. He said in his old age:

I do not know what I may seem to the world, but, as to myself, I seem to have been only like a boy playing on the sea shore, and diverting myself in now and then finding a smoother pebble or a prettier shell than ordinary, whilst the great ocean of truth lay all undiscovered before me.

BIOLOGY AND BOTANY
Meanwhile, in the Netherlands Anton van Leeuwenhoek (1632–1723) was making important discoveries with the microscope. He used this to find out how parts of the human body are made up, including blood, muscle, hair and skin.

Carl Linné (1707–1778), or Linnaeus, was a Swedish *botanist* who worked out a scientific system of identifying plants and animals and dividing them into different groups. His system is still used today.

THE SCIENTIFIC WORLD
Other scientists in Europe at this time were studying astronomy, mathematics, chemistry, medicine, engineering and physics. It was an exciting time.

Right. The Eddystone Lighthouse was built on rocks in the English Channel near Plymouth. The first one was built of wood and was swept away in a storm in 1703. The second lighthouse was burnt down in 1755. By this time trading in ships was so important to Britain that a new and better design was needed. John Smeaton had already made improvements to water mills and windmills and so he was asked to design and build the next lighthouse in 1759. This time the design was so good that the lighthouse withstood all storms until 1882, when it was found that the rocks it was built on were cracking.

Some Discoveries between 1650 and 1700

1665 Robert Hooke, of England, uses an early microscope to look at a piece of cork and becomes the first person to see cells
1666 Newton forms his theory of gravity
1669 Hennig Brand of Hamburg in Germany isolates the element phosphorous
1675 Dutch scientist, Anton van Leeuwenhoek, improves the microscope so that it can magnify an object 200 times and discovers microscopic organisms
1690 Papin, a French engineer, invents a pump with a piston driven by steam
1698 Hunckwitz produces the first phosphorous matches

Above. Anton van Leeuwenhoek.

Some Discoveries between 1700 and 1800

1715 German physicist, Gabriel Fahrenheit, introduces the mercury thermometer
1731 John Hadley invents an early type of sextant, used to measure the angle above the horizon of the sun or the stars, and so help sailors to find their position at sea
1742 Celsius invents the centigrade thermometer in Sweden
1746 American writer, scientist and politician Benjamin Franklin begins his researches into electricity which prove that it causes lightning
1753 Carl Linnaeus, a Swedish botanist, publishes his new system for grouping plants

Below. Isaac Newton took his degree at Cambridge University in 1665. Within months the university was closed because of the plague and

Newton went home to live with his mother. He worked on theories about splitting light and about the law of gravity.

Above. This chronometer, designed by John Harrison, kept very accurate time and helped sailors to fix their longitude.

1761 Mikhail Lomonosov, the founder of Moscow University, discovers that the planet Venus has an atmosphere
1765 James Watt improves Thomas Newcomen's pumping engine
1774 Joseph Priestley, a British scientist, discovers oxygen and Karl Scheele, a Swedish scientist, discovers chlorine
1783 The Montgolfier brothers, of France, make the first hot air balloon ascent
1786 British astronomer Sir William Herschel forms the theory of the shape of a galaxy
1789 An Italian, Luigi Galvani, experiments on the muscular contractions of dead frogs
1790 French scientist Antoine Lavoisier produces the first table of chemical elements

Above. Newton's first reflecting telescope. He used mirrors to overcome the lack of good quality glass lenses.

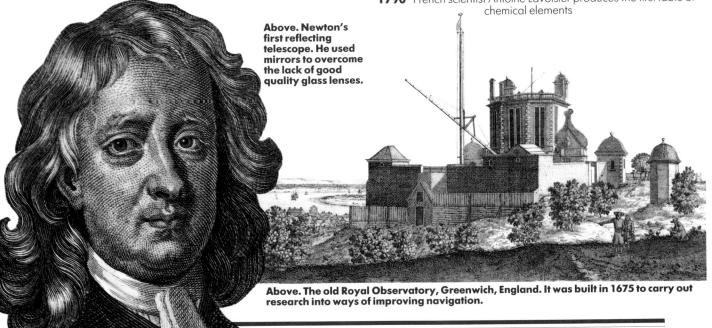

Above. The old Royal Observatory, Greenwich, England. It was built in 1675 to carry out research into ways of improving navigation.

THE ART OF WAR

Europe developed the art and equipment of warfare to a high degree in the seventeenth and eighteenth centuries. One reason for this was the change in the organization of armies.

PERMANENT ARMIES Almost constant warfare in the 100 years before 1650 had left parts of Europe, such as the German states, devastated. It had also become obvious that permanent armies were useful, as previously armies were only raised when wars broke out.

By 1650, France was the leading military power in Europe. Its kings, particularly Louis XIV (see p. 22) and his ministers, realized that a strong army would keep France powerful. However, if France began to set up a large army, then every other monarch in Europe also had to keep a large army. This was a seventeenth century arms race.

THE SIZE OF ARMIES In 1610, France's army was made up of about 20,000 soldiers; in 1650, there were 150,000; during the eighteenth century this number rose to 250,000 and more in time of war. In the same way, Sweden's army was 15,000-strong in 1590 and 100,000 in 1700.

Above. The Battle of Culloden, 1746. Bonnie Prince Charlie (1720–1788) came to Scotland to proclaim his father, James Stuart, the true king of Britain. He gathered an army and marched south to Derby before turning back to Scotland and being defeated at Culloden.

In the seventeenth century a soldier on horseback wore much the same armor as a pike-man (far left), who went on foot. He had a helmet, breastplate, backplate and some protection for the thighs. The musketeer (left) was the first soldier to do without armor, for with his musket and gunpowder he had enough to carry without it.

The Development of Navies

In many countries, there were merchants who hired ships to sail long or short distances to buy and sell goods. Europeans in particular built large ships and sailed great distances to trade. They needed to protect their ships from pirates who might attack and steal their goods, so often their merchant ships were armed.

Special sailing ships were built by countries like the Netherlands, France, Spain and Britain. These were warships, built to fight battles at sea and protect their countries' interests, defend their trade and help to build empires.

At this time, the warships were armed with cannons along the side of the ship; the cannons were fired through open portholes.

Matchlocks and Flintlocks

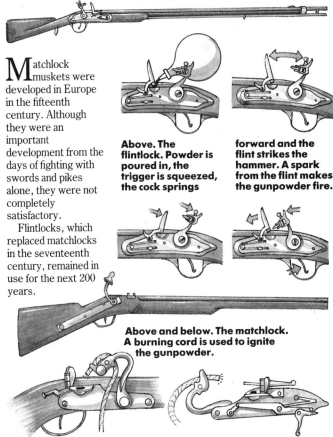

Matchlock muskets were developed in Europe in the fifteenth century. Although they were an important development from the days of fighting with swords and pikes alone, they were not completely satisfactory.

Flintlocks, which replaced matchlocks in the seventeenth century, remained in use for the next 200 years.

Above. The flintlock. Powder is poured in, the trigger is squeezed, the cock springs

forward and the flint strikes the hammer. A spark from the flint makes the gunpowder fire.

Above and below. The matchlock. A burning cord is used to ignite the gunpowder.

GUNS Perhaps the greatest breakthrough on the battlefield was the development of a new type of early gun, the flintlock musket.

With the old matchlock musket, a *musketeer* (soldier who used the gun) had to pour loose gunpowder into the weapon and then detonate it with a smoldering cord. It was very slow to load and could easily misfire. The new flintlock meant that the gunpowder (which came in measured paper cartridges) was ignited by a spark from the flint. This usually worked reliably and in all weathers. Loading was much faster, so there was far more firepower available on the battlefield.

More firepower meant the end of armor on the battlefield. Once bayonets were fixed to the barrels of the muskets, not so many *pike-men* were needed to keep off *cavalry* attacks. Within a short space of time more soldiers were armed with guns than with anything else.

PROFESSIONAL ARMIES Armies gradually became more professional. Better weapons needed better soldiers. It was no use recruiting peasants in times of war, giving them complicated guns and then expecting them to be good soldiers. More and more soldiers were now employed full-time. They drilled and trained. They were given uniforms, weapons and, in some countries, even health-care and pensions. All this meant that large government departments grew up to clothe, arm, control and feed the armies. The monarchs were strong enough to take the control of regiments of soldiers away from the nobles, who had previously been in charge. The nobles remained as officers and still did some recruiting, but the army was now the army of the monarch.

PRUSSIA Frederick William I of Prussia (1713–1740) built up a well-equipped, disciplined army. It was his pride and joy. He had scouts sent all over Europe to find the tallest young men (they did not have to be Prussian) to serve in his army. If they could not be persuaded to join, he was not above kidnapping them. The problem was that he did not like risking any of them in fighting. His son, Frederick the Great (see p. 22), was more practical. He improved the training of soldiers and set about conquering more land to make Prussia the most powerful of the many German states.

NAVIES Similar widescale changes took place in the navies. The British navy grew in size, professionalism and firepower and led to British dominance at sea.

THE COMING OF INDUSTRY: COAL AND IRON

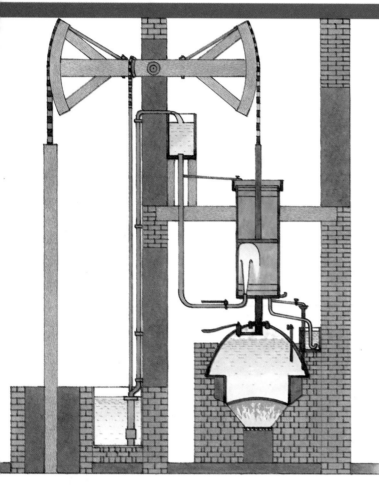

Above. Newcomen's engine was used to pump water out of mines. The boiler at the bottom right heated the water to make steam, which rose **into the cylinder. A jet of cold water was injected into the cylinder. The steam condensed. As it became cooler, it took up less room than the steam had** **and so a vacuum was created. The piston dropped down, pulling down the arch head on the big wooden beam, which lifted the water.**

The foundations of present-day European industry were laid in the eighteenth century with the development of new machinery and processes that is known as the Industrial Revolution. Although these new developments soon spread all over Europe, it was in Britain that most of them originated.

BRITAIN AND THE INDUSTRIAL REVOLUTION

In 1700, Britain had large reserves of coal and plenty of iron ore. However, that alone does not make an industrial revolution. Britain had other advantages too. The first was that the country had been united for a long time. Monarchs came and went, but the government carried on

through Parliament. This provided a stable background in which business could flourish.

Another advantage was that Britain was an island, so the wars that raged throughout Europe in the sixteenth and seventeenth centuries did not touch its countryside. These wars were devastating in places like the German states, where large amounts of land were laid to waste.

Yet another advantage was that during the eighteenth century Britain was expanding overseas and gaining a great deal of money from trade, so that some British people had the capital (money) to invest in new ideas such as canal-building, cotton factories and steam engineering.

In some ways the country that seemed to have the most advantages, however, was China. China was a united, stable empire with (like Britain) many skilled workers in agricultural and structural engineering. The difference between Britain and China seems to have been their different attitudes. The British belonged to Europe. They had taken part in world explorations. They were among the pioneers of scientific thinking. They were part of the outward-looking, progressive and wealth-seeking European climate of the eighteenth century. The Chinese, on the other hand, saw themselves as the Middle Kingdom—the center of the world. They did not need the rest of the world.

So the small, united, peaceful and relatively rich land of Britain experienced the first industrial revolution, soon to be followed by other countries and eventually by a great deal of the world.

NEW DEVELOPMENTS

This industrial revolution was made possible by new discoveries in science and engineering. For instance, Abraham Darby (1677–1717) pioneered the use of coked coal to smelt iron ore. For the first time good quality iron could be produced. Large quantities of high-quality iron were needed to make the new machines and steam engines that men like Thomas Newcomen (1663–1729) and James Watt (1736–1819) were inventing, while large quantities of coal were needed to power them.

WOOL AND COTTON INDUSTRIES

At first the steam engine was stationary. It was used to pump water out of the deep mines. Then people realized that it could be used to drive machines. For instance, previously the mills that wove wool had to be sited by fast-flowing rivers

Left. Wrought iron is strong and supple. It was popular in the eighteenth century for things like balcony railings outside town houses. One common pattern was called "heart and honeysuckle."

The staircase above and fireplace below are made of wrought iron.

1 In 1756 a factory was built at Sèvres in northern France to make porcelain. This followed the factory at Meissen in eastern Germany earlier in the century. At last the Europeans had discovered for themselves the Chinese secret of making the very fine china called porcelain.

2 The Chinese did not want the Europeans to gain too much influence in their country. In 1757 they insisted that all foreign ships that wanted to trade with China, had to be restricted to the port of Canton.

3 The Portuguese unified their South American empire in 1776. It was to be ruled from Rio de Janiero (in present-day Brazil).

4 In 1770 James Bruce became the first white person to journey along the Blue Nile to where it joined the White Nile.

Left. The iron bridge at Coalbrookdale, Shropshire, in England was the first iron bridge in the world. The iron ribs of the arches are 67 meters long.

Below. The Coalbrookdale Ironworks in the eighteenth century. Steam engines drove the bellows that kept the ironworks going day and night.

Children being let down a coal mine. They worked long hours, pulling tubs of coal, crawling on hands and knees along underground passages. Six-year-olds sat for hours in the dark to open the doors as the tubs were pulled along. In 1842, Britain forbade women and children under the age of 10 to work underground.

so that the water could power the machines. By the late eighteenth century this was no longer so. Woollen mills and the newer cotton mills could be built anywhere if the power source was a steam engine rather than water.

This led to the building of cotton mills in Lancashire. They were near the coal fields, so it was easy to bring coal to the steam engines in the mills, and they were also near the ports of Liverpool and Manchester, where cotton was brought in from India, Egypt and America and from where the finished cotton cloth was exported all over the world. All these developments meant that Britain's industry, trade and wealth were able to grow enormously.

THE COMING OF INDUSTRY: COTTON AND TRANSPORT

In 1650, wool and flax were the main raw materials that were used to make clothes in Britain. Small amounts of silk from China and cotton from India were imported for rich people.

By the eighteenth century, however, printed cotton cloth (calico) from India was becoming so popular in Britain that the government banned its import. This was to protect the small but growing British cotton industry in Manchester. At this time the cotton mills only made crude copies of the Indian calicoes, but as the eighteenth century progressed the quality of their cloth improved. More and more people wanted dresses, shirts and so on made out of cotton, because they were lighter to wear and easier to wash than woollen clothes.

Left. A Spinning Jenny. The cotton fibers were combed out in the wooden "bed." They were then picked up by one of the many spindles on the spinning wheel.

Below. A working mill. Until the invention of steam-powered machines at the end of the eighteenth century, factories and mills were built near fast-flowing rivers. The water turned a waterwheel, which provided the power for all the machines. You can see the large waterwheel in the center of this picture. Notice all the women working. The man in the top hat is overseeing the work.

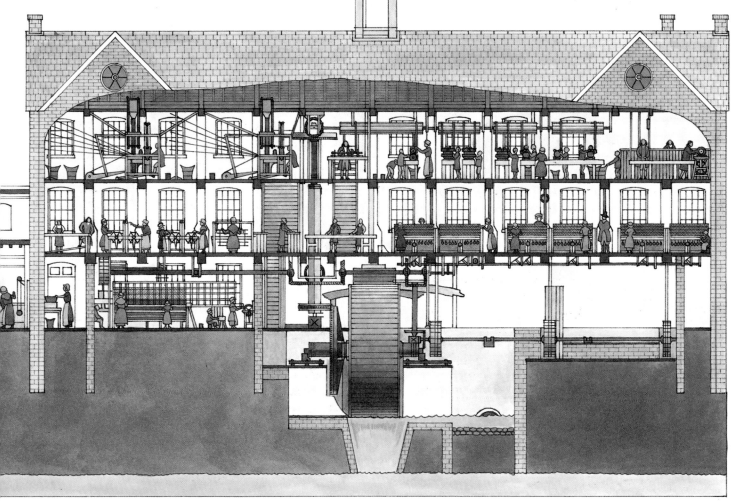

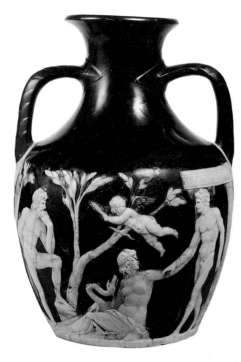

The Dangers of Highwaymen

Highwaymen were a menace on the roads during this period. Some famous robbers in Britain were Moll Cutpurse, who held up coaches dressed as a man, and Dick Turpin, who was finally hanged in 1739.

Stagecoaches were held up so often that in 1784 a new service was tried out between London and Bath. It was called the Mail Coach and it was accompanied by an armed guard. Soon there were mail coaches running from London to all the cities in Britain.

The Growth of Canals

The first efforts to improve water transport were attempts to widen, deepen and straighten rivers, to allow boats to get further inland. This helped trade because more heavy goods could be carried by water, as packhorses could only carry fairly small loads.

Straightening rivers was so successful that people decided to build artificial rivers. They were called canals. By the end of the eighteenth century there were canals all over Britain.

Above. The Portland Vase is a Roman vase made of glass with white figures on it. The figures are slightly raised, and stand out from the surface of the vase. This gave Wedgwood the idea of making his blue pottery with raised white figures on it.

JAMES HARGREAVES, RICHARD ARKWRIGHT AND THE MULE The people who span the long threads from the raw cotton could not work fast enough to keep up with the increased demand. To overcome this problem, James Hargreaves (1720–1778) invented the *Spinning Jenny*, a machine which span eight threads at once.

Shortly afterwards, Richard Arkwright (1732–1792) pioneered the *water-frame*. This brought great changes. It was too heavy to be turned by hand and so it was driven by a water-wheel. This meant that, instead of working at home, spinners now went to work in mills that were built beside rivers. These were some of the earliest factories, which changed people's working lives beyond recognition.

Then, in the 1780s, Samuel Crompton (1753–1827) invented another new machine, called the *mule*, which could spin cotton threads as fine as any from India, and far more cheaply.

MANCHESTER AND COTTON The next change in the production of cotton came when the steam engine was used for power instead of the waterwheel. Now that mills did not have to be built by rivers, they appeared all over Manchester, not far from the port of Liverpool, where raw cotton arrived in huge bales from Turkey and India. Soon the cotton imported from these countries was not enough to supply all the mills, and so Britain turned to the *New World*. Cotton grew well in the southern states of North America, where plantation

owners began to grow cotton by the square mile, using their slaves to grow and then pick the cotton. This cotton was shipped to Liverpool and sent from there by canal to Manchester.

CANALS AND ROADS In the second half of the eighteenth century, the Duke of Bridgewater built the first canal, 68 kilometers long, to link his coal mines with Manchester. It had cost him £2 a ton to transport his coal by road, but now, by canal, it cost only 50p a ton. Because he saved so much money in this way, the duke could afford to sell his coal more cheaply than other mine-owners could, and so more people bought his coal. Other mine-owners followed his example and soon canals were being built all over Britain.

Josiah Wedgwood (1730–1795), the famous pottery manufacturer, used canals to transport his pottery from the Midlands to London. This was cheaper than sending it by road and also meant that the pottery was less likely to break.

Roads were improved, too. In 1658, it took 96 hours to travel from London to Exeter, while in 1784 the new Royal Mail coach could do it in 32 hours.

Britain now had everything that was needed for full industrial take-off—raw materials (coal, iron, cotton), power (water, steam) and transport (canals, roads). Soon steam would be applied to transport and the huge industrial expansion of the nineteenth century would begin.

Changes in Europe
TIME CHART

AD	BRITAIN	FRANCE	RUSSIA	REST OF EUROPE
1656				Completion of the building of St. Peter's in Rome
1660	Foundation of the Royal Society in London			
1660>1700		Classical period of French literature: Molière, Racine, Corneille		
1662		Louis XIV begins building Versailles		
1666	Great Fire of London kills over 60,000	Foundation of Académie Française in Paris		
1683				Turkish siege of Vienna
1687	Isaac Newton's *Principia* published			
1696			Peter the Great takes full control in Russia	
1700		Great period of European Enlightenment begins: Voltaire, Diderot, Hume, etc.		Great age of German Baroque music begins: Bach, Handel, Buxtehude, etc.
1701	Jethro Tull invents horsedrawn drill to plant seeds in rows			
1703			Foundation of the city of St. Petersburg	
1709	Abraham Darby discovers coke-smelting technique to produce pig-iron		Peter the Great defeats the Swedes at the battle of Poltava	
1710	Christopher Wren's St. Paul's Cathedral is completed			Meissen porcelain industry is established in Saxony
1719			Jesuits expelled from Russia	
1724			Scientific Academy set up in St. Petersburg	
1725			Death of Peter the Great	Prague Opera House is established in Czechoslovakia
1742				Celsius invents the centigrade thermometer
1743		French explorers reach the foothills of the Rocky Mountains in North America		
1747	Samuel Johnson plans the first dictionary of the English language			
1757	The first modern British canal is constructed in Lancashire			
1764	James Hargreaves invents the Spinning Jenny			Mozart produces his first symphony at the age of eight
1765	James Watt refines the steam engine			
1781			Siberian highway is begun	
1783		Montgolfier brothers make the first balloon ascent	Russia annexes Crimea	
1789		French Revolution begins		
1790				Great age of European orchestral music: Haydn, Beethoven, Mozart, etc.
1791			Russia gains Black Sea steppes from Turkey	
1799		Napoleon becomes First Consul		

Spanish possessions

Portuguese possessions

British possessions

French possessions

Dutch possessions

Danish possessions

PART TWO

Revolution and Empire

Until the seventeenth century the world, on the whole, had pressed in on Europe. From 1650 on, Europe pressed out on the world. China had been the most civilized, advanced and densely populated country in the world in 1500. By 1650, however, the Chinese were losing interest in the outside world and in new things. The Europeans, on the other hand, were looking outwards from Europe. The first wave of explorations was over and the time of European trade and settlement was beginning.

GLOBAL TRADE European ships sailed to the East Indies, India, the West Indies, Africa and North and South America. They traded in everything, from spices to slaves, from silver to sugar, setting up trading posts around the world. The Dutch had trading posts in the East Indies, the Portuguese in Africa, the British and French in India. Different races of people, and different animals and plants, were spreading around the globe. This was to have far-reaching effects.

SETTLEMENT After trade came settlement. In the Americas the native populations declined by about 90 percent, due firstly to the violence of the new settlers towards them, and secondly to new diseases that the settlers brought with them. The native American peoples were replaced by white Europeans, black Africans and some mixed races. This was to be the most significant world change in the distribution of races, taking place over two or three centuries. By the nineteenth century, trade and settlement had an overwhelming effect on every human life on earth.

At the same time, Eurasian animals such as horses, cows and sheep were introduced to the Americas, while plants like the potato and maize were introduced from the Americas to Eurasia. These changes, too, affected people's lives dramatically.

THE DESIRE FOR TRADE The hunter-gatherer societies had everything they wanted. Many of them were *nomadic* or semi-nomadic. If you are always on the move, then possessions are a burden. Only when people settled down to farm and stay in one place did they discover the need for chairs and tables, for bowls, beds, sheets, changes of clothes, pictures, ornaments and so on. Trade grew up from the desire to own things. Someone else living a mile away or 1000 miles away always seemed to have something that was very desirable.

In this way trade grew up everywhere and more and more ships plied back and forth across the oceans of the world.

An Era of Revolution

THE THIRTEEN COLONIES OF NORTH AMERICA

By the seventeenth century, European settlers in the Americas had defeated the native Americans and the British had emerged in control of the eastern seaboard of North America.

The 13 British colonies hugged the east coast, stretching inland only for about 240 kilometers. For a long time, any further expansion was prevented by the mountains to the west, beyond which lay lands unexplored by white people, where the *Amerindian* peoples had lived for thousands of years. The European settlers wanted this land, and there were bound to be clashes as the new farmers cut down forests for timber and to make fields, because these were the forests where the Amerindians hunted.

LIFE IN THE COLONIES In 1690, about 200,000 settlers lived in the 13 colonies. Although most of them were British settlers (many Scottish and Irish), there were also Swedish, Dutch and German people, together with French Huguenots who had fled from persecution in

The Thirteen Colonies

NEW HAMPSHIRE
MASSACHUSETTS
NEW YORK
RHODE ISLAND
CONNECTICUT
PENNSYLVANIA
NEW JERSEY
PHILADELPHIA
MARYLAND
DELAWARE
VIRGINIA
BALTIMORE

FRENCH LOUISIANA

N. CAROLINA

S. CAROLINA

ATLANTIC OCEAN

GEORGIA

SPANISH FLORIDA

Above. Map showing the thirteen colonies in North America in the eighteenth century.

Catholic France.

A large number of religious English people had settled in the part of America that became known as New England. They wanted to live and worship God in a simple and pure way and because of this they were often known as *Puritans*. Their wooden houses were clustered around village greens, and each village had a meeting house for worship and where people could meet to discuss community affairs. The settlers wanted a just and free society for everyone, with people meeting together to decide how best to run the community. They were very strict about religious matters, but otherwise they wanted people to be equal and free in this new land. Near to the village green there was a house for the minister, and perhaps also a small school house where all the children would go. The settlers themselves lived by farming, fishing and trading in furs and timber.

Further south, in Maryland,

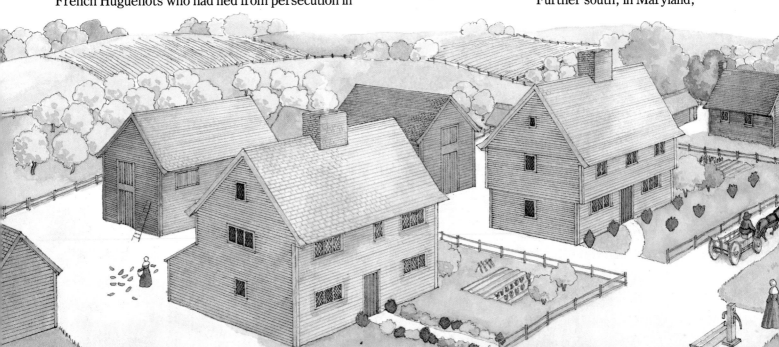

The scene above shows William Penn, who founded Pennsylvania, making a treaty with the Indians.

most of the settlers were Catholic. Neighboring Pennsylvania was founded by *Quakers*, who were also religious people who wanted to live simply. They were hardworking people who farmed and tried to live in peace with the local Indians.

In the southernmost parts of North America, religion was not so predominant. The land here was good for farming crops like tobacco and cotton. Since there was a demand for both these products in Europe, trading settlements soon grew up along the coasts.

THE NEW CITIES The city of Philadelphia was founded in 1681 and by 1750 it was the busiest port in America.

Baltimore was slower to grow. In 1752, it had only 25 houses and 200 people, but in the next 50 years it became a huge center for exporting wheat and for shipping. Goods were sent from ports like these to Europe and to the West Indies.

BRITAIN, SPAIN AND FRANCE By the early eighteenth century, there were around 900,000 British settlers in North America. There were also about 5000 Spanish and 50,000 French settlers in colonies founded by Spain and France. The Spanish were not interested in expanding their colonies in Mexico, Florida and California, but it was a different matter with the French.

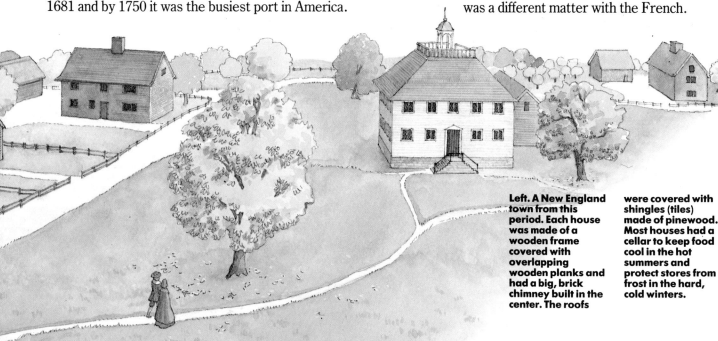

Left. A New England town from this period. Each house was made of a wooden frame covered with overlapping wooden planks and had a big, brick chimney built in the center. The roofs were covered with shingles (tiles) made of pinewood. Most houses had a cellar to keep food cool in the hot summers and protect stores from frost in the hard, cold winters.

THE FRENCH AND BRITISH IN NORTH AMERICA

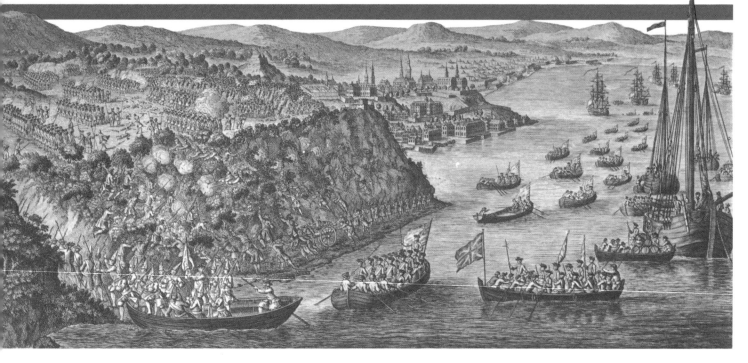

Above. A view of the British army taking Quebec in October 1759. The British soldiers are seen disembarking and climbing up the cliff to fight the French.

By the early eighteenth century, there were 50,000 French settlers in North America, who had gained a vast amount of land on the other side of the mountains from the British colonies in New England. The French lived mostly as hunters and fur traders, on friendly terms with the Amerindians, because there were not enough French settlers to make much difference to the local people's way of life. The British, on the other hand, having a much larger colony of 900,000 people, wanted to cross the mountains to gain more land. When they did this they clashed not only with the Amerindians, but with the French as well, who built a line of forts to stop the British advancing.

The French not only wanted to stop the British colony expanding, they wanted to expand too, looking towards the sea and the possibility of attacking the British along the river towards New York. So, in turn, the British built forts to stop them. From the late seventeenth century onwards, war in Europe between France and Britain was reflected by almost continuous warfare between the French and British settlers in North America.

WASHINGTON AND BRADDOCK The first clash came in 1754, when the British colony of Virginia felt

George Washington (1732–99)

When Washington was 11 years old, his father died and his step-brother brought him up. After this brother died, Washington ran the family estates. When he was in his 20s he led soldiers for the British against the French who were attacking the colonies.

Washington represented his fellow landowners in the Virginia parliament, and when trouble flared up between the British and the American colonists he was given the job of recruiting and leading an army made up of farmhands and craftsmen. This amateur army kept the British forces occupied until the French joined the Americans in 1778 and forced the British to surrender at Yorktown in 1781. Washington was the first president of the new independent states of America, from 1789 to 1797.

threatened by a strong French fort on the Ohio River. Virginia only had a *militia* (part-time army), but a tall, confident, 21 year-old militia officer called George Washington (see p. 48) persuaded the governor of Virginia to send him with 159 men against the French fort. Although he captured the fort, Washington had to surrender it later.

The next year an army of British soldiers, led by

Changing Ownership of North America, 1713–1763

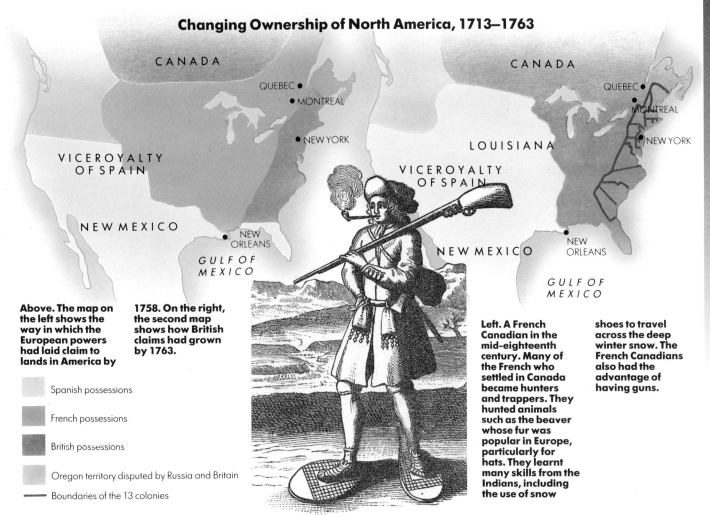

Above. The map on the left shows the way in which the European powers had laid claim to lands in America by

1758. On the right, the second map shows how British claims had grown by 1763.

Spanish possessions

French possessions

British possessions

Oregon territory disputed by Russia and Britain

Boundaries of the 13 colonies

Left. A French Canadian in the mid-eighteenth century. Many of the French who settled in Canada became hunters and trappers. They hunted animals such as the beaver whose fur was popular in Europe, particularly for hats. They learnt many skills from the Indians, including the use of snow shoes to travel across the deep winter snow. The French Canadians also had the advantage of having guns.

Key Dates in the British-French Dispute

1750	British-French commission fails to agree boundaries
1753	George Washington is sent on mission to tell the French not to confront the British
1754	British troops sent to expel French
1755	French and Indian War against Britain
1756	French drive British from the Great Lakes. The opening of the Seven Years War
1758	British take Louisburg
1759	Spain joins France in war against Britain
1759	British take Quebec
1760	British win control of the St. Lawrence River and gain Montreal
1761	British dominate West Indies
1762	Britain declares war on Spain and takes more West Indian islands
1763	Peace of Paris between Britain, France and Spain ends the Seven Years' War.

General Braddock, was easily defeated by the French. Braddock himself was mortally wounded. The French went over to the attack, taking all the British forts guarding the way to New York, and it looked as if nothing could stop them.

THE SEVEN YEARS' WAR However, the war in America was only one part of the larger conflict between the French and British for world power. Because this conflict stretched all over the world, the role played by their ships and navies was very important.

In 1756, the Seven Years' War diverted the French towards fighting in Europe. The British seized their chance. British ships controlled the sea routes across the Atlantic Ocean and did not allow French ships to reach America. This meant that the French forts were starved of soldiers, food and ammunition.

The British took Louisburg in Canada in 1758 and moved on Quebec next. General Wolfe was put in charge of the British army. He sailed up the St. Lawrence River with a few thousand soldiers, who entered Quebec secretly in the night and defeated the French army. In 1760 the British captured Montreal too.

THE PEACE OF PARIS, 1763 This treaty ended the Seven Years' War and was a great defeat for France. Britain gained all the French possessions east of the Mississippi River, except New Orleans, while the territory to the west was granted to Spain. Britain also gained Florida from the Spanish (although this was returned 18 years later) and, on the other side of the world, made gains from the French in India, giving up some West Indian islands in return.

THE BOSTON TEA PARTY

The painting above shows the Boston Tea Party. Some of the colonists disguised themselves as Indians and threw the tea overboard in protest against British taxes.

Soon after the British had defeated the French in the Seven Years' War, they were in trouble with their own North American colonists. By 1770, there were about two million people living in the 13 colonies. Large ports, like Boston and New York, were growing rich on trading.

Moreover, as the eighteenth century wore on the colonies developed in their own ways. They were governed by the British king's governor and council, but power really lay with the elected assemblies in the colonies themselves. They ran their own affairs 3000 miles away from Britain. They prospered and made most of the manufactured goods they needed. They were fast becoming Americans.

NAVIGATION LAWS The colonists resented the British Navigation Laws, which protected British trade and ship-building. For instance, the colonies were only allowed to trade with Britain and all goods had to be carried in British ships.

STAMP DUTY On the other hand, the British had used their army to fight off the French. They felt it was only fair that the colonists should pay some money in taxes

Key Dates leading to the Declaration of Independence

1765	The Stamp Act
1766	Repeal of the Stamp Act
1770	New taxes on items such as tea lead to unrest and to British soldiers killing four colonists
1773	Boston Tea Party
1775	Concord raid and battle at Lexington Heavy British losses at Bunker Hill
1776	American Declaration of Independence

towards the cost of defending the colonies, and so they decided to raise taxes by means of a stamp duty, a tax on legal documents. The colonists were furious. They claimed the stamp duty was illegal, saying that the very reason that British people were freer than most other peoples in Europe was they they could not be taxed unless it had been agreed in Parliament, whose Members were elected by at least some of the British population. The Americans said that they had not voted for any Members of Parliament in London, so how could those Members put taxes on them? There was such a protest that the British repealed the stamp duty.

Left. The *Spirit of '76*, the American Revolution painting by A.M. Willard. The picture shows the revolutionaries carrying the flag of the 13 colonies, who now called themselves "states." In the blue square there is one white star for each new state. Since 1776 many states have joined the United States and each time another white star has been added to the flag.

1 The Quebec Act guaranteed Roman Catholics freedom to worship in Canada. This angered the Puritans in New England.

2 The Treaty of Kuchuk Kainardji ended the Russo-Turkish War. Russia gained ports on the Black Sea from Turkey and also the right to represent the Greek Orthodox Church in Turkey.

3 Britain forbade cotton-making machinery made in that country to be exported anywhere in the world. This was to prevent the cotton industries of other countries developing into rivals of the British cotton industry.

4 The Austrian doctor Franz Anton Mesmer first used hypnosis for health purposes in Vienna.

Paul Revere (1735–1818) was one of the Boston leaders of the revolt against the British. He took part in the Boston Tea Party. When the revolt began, the British set out to seize the American military stores at Concord, Massachusetts. Revere learned of the plan and on April 18, 1775 he galloped through the night waking the people, so that when the British approached Concord the next day there were armed men to meet them. The story is told in a poem by the American poet, Longfellow, in *Paul Revere's Ride*.

THE BOSTON TEA PARTY Instead, the British said duties (taxes) must be paid on goods such as tea. The colonists did not like this either and the British sent soldiers to keep order in Boston. Tempers went from bad to worse. In 1773, a group of 150 colonists boarded three ships in Boston Harbor and threw all the tea overboard. The British put Boston under a military governor, General Gage, and closed the port of Boston until the colonists paid a fine.

From this time on, the colonists and the British were moving towards an open conflict. The Americans did not see this as a revolution. Rather, they thought the British were acting like illegal tyrants. Most Americans had no wish at this time to break away and become an independent country, they just wished to be free to grow and prosper in their own way. Some people in Britain sympathized with the Americans, as the thinkers of the Enlightenment (see pp. 30–31) had made people aware of the rights of others. These rights did not include slaves or women, but at least the idea was a beginning of thoughts about freedom and democracy. However, the British government stood firm. If the colonists were allowed to get away with it this time, then they could defy Britain over anything. Each side decided to stand firm.

THE AMERICAN DECLARATION OF INDEPENDENCE

North America in 1783

British

United States

Spanish

Russian

Unclaimed

Map showing the lands of the new United States of America in 1783 and the lands in North and Central America that were claimed by the European powers. Much of the Spanish lands north of Mexico were passed to France in the 1790s and were sold to the United States in 1803.

In July 1775, representatives from all 13 rebel colonies met at Philadelphia and asked George Washington (1732–1799) to take command of the Patriot army. After this, fighting between the British and the colonists dragged on. The following year the representatives met again and on 4th July they agreed to adopt the Declaration of Independence.

This Declaration was drafted by Thomas Jefferson (1743–1826) and others. It explained simply the American complaints against George III, the king of Britain. Then it went on to describe the sort of government the Americans wanted to set up, which was much influenced by the ideas of the Enlightenment (see pp. 30–31).

EQUALITY The Declaration said that all men were created equal. Governments were set up to make sure that ordinary people could live safely, freely and happily. If they failed to protect this freedom, the ordinary people had the right to throw out the government and set up a new one. The British, however, had no intention of accepting such a document.

THE WAR OF INDEPENDENCE It was one thing to declare independence, another to break free of the British. In 1775, when the American War of Independence began, there were 8500 British soldiers in America; by 1781, there were over 48,000. They were professional, disciplined soldiers. The American militia, however, were part-time soldiers, keen to fight, but also keen to go back to their farms to get the harvest in.

WASHINGTON George Washington was commander of the new American Continental Army. At its best, it numbered about 20,000 men in 1777, but numbers went up and down as men signed up for a few months and then went home.

Over the next few years, despite some British victories, Washington trained and disciplined his men. While they shaped into an efficient army, the British faced more and more difficulties. All their guns, horses and food had to be brought 3000 miles across the Atlantic Ocean from Britain. Often the army leaders were not very good. One of the British generals was "Gentleman" Johnny Burgoyne, who was more interested in the cases

The New Constitution

The 13 colonies had worked together to fight the British, but Washington and others realized that the new states would be stronger if they made a formal agreement to act together. For instance, it had been very difficult to get all 13 to pay taxes to pay for the soldiers. In another war this might be disastrous.

A new constitution was drawn up and the people in each of the 13 states were asked to vote to agree to it. In some states the voting was very close. In Virginia, 89 were for the constitution and 79 against.

The new constitution used the British idea of protecting the individual person by dividing up the powers of the state, so that no single person (e.g., the president) or group of people (e.g., the judges) would be so powerful that they could become absolute rulers. There was to be a president, two legislative houses (sets of people voted in to make laws) and an independent group of judges who could not be told what to do by the legislative houses.

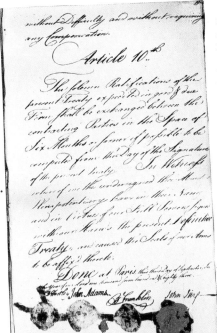

Left. One of the Articles of the Treaty of Paris signed between the British and Americans to end the war.

Key People apart from Washington

Right. Alexander Hamilton (*c.* 1755–1804) started work at the age of 11 in a counting house in New York. He fought against the British in the War of Independence. He later trained as a lawyer and was Secretary of the Treasury after independence, helping to build a strong central government for the new United States.

Left. The British forces led by Cornwallis surrendering to Washington and the French at Yorktown. In 1783 Washington entered New York and the British finally recognized the independence of the 13 states. The rest of the British soldiers went home.

Below. John Adams (1735–1826), a lawyer, helped to draw up the Declaration of Independence. He was the second president of the US and the first to live in the White House.

Left. Benjamin Franklin (1706–90) was an inventor, writer and thinker. In 1776 he joined with Jefferson and others to draft the Declaration of Independence. After the war, he helped to draft the new constitution for the United States.

Above. Thomas Jefferson (1743–1826) was a lawyer and politician who helped to draft the Declaration of Independence. He was an ambassador in Europe during the War of Independence. Jefferson was later president of the United States of America from 1800 to 1808.

of champagne he had brought with him than in leading his men in battle. He was forced to surrender to the Americans at the Battle of Saratoga in 1777.

BENJAMIN FRANKLIN AND THE FRENCH The war continued. Then Benjamin Franklin (1706–1790), a clever American diplomat, persuaded the French that the Americans would win. The French, seeing a chance to get back some of the land they had lost to Britain after the Seven Years' War (see p. 45), entered the war on the side of the colonists. By 1781, Spain and the Netherlands had joined in as well, also against Britain, and the small colonial war had become a world war. The combined navies of France, Spain and the Netherlands made it even more difficult for food and guns to reach the British soldiers in America.

THE END OF THE WAR The end came suddenly. Washington gathered an army of 16,000 American and French soldiers and hemmed in the British army at Yorktown in Virginia. The British General Cornwallis surrendered. In 1783 Britain was thoroughly defeated and signed a treaty at Versailles in France agreeing that America was now independent.

The soldier pictured furthest to the left is an American soldier from George Washington's army. Next to him, to the right of the picture, is a British soldier.

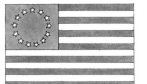

Above. The flag of the newly independent 13 states. Each star and red and white stripe represents a state. As more states joined, so more stars were added to the flag, but the number of stripes remained the same to represent the original 13.

THE FRENCH REVOLUTION

By 1789, France was a collection of provinces which had been brought together as one country. Each had its own customs, styles of clothing and even laws. Louis XIV (see p. 22) had been a very strong king and had held all the provinces together. The next two kings were weak and, under their kingship, the problems of an old-fashioned country began to show.

CLERGY, PEASANTS AND NOBLES The adult population of France in the late eighteenth century was about 25 million. Only one million of these were nobles and clergy, but the clergy alone owned one-fifth of all the land in France. Most of the rest was owned by the nobles or the king.

The peasants worked from dawn to dusk on land owned by their local lord. Taxes to the king were high as a result of the wars that France had fought in the seventeenth and eighteenth centuries, and because of the extravagance of Louis XIV and Louis XV. In addition, all peasants had to pay a tithe (tenth) of what they earned to the clergy. The nobles and clergy, on the other hand,

Above. The storming of the Bastille on July 14, 1789. The French revolutionaries saw the Bastille as a great symbol of the king and the government.

Left. A French general from the king's army stands furthest to the left. Next to him is a soldier of the Revolution, called a *sans culotte* because he wore trousers instead of knee breeches.

The Guillotine

The guillotine was used for all executions after 1792. It was part of the revolutionaries' idea of equality that all people were executed in the same way. The guillotine was named after Joseph Ignace Guillotin, who supported the idea of making executions quick and painless.

France in 1789

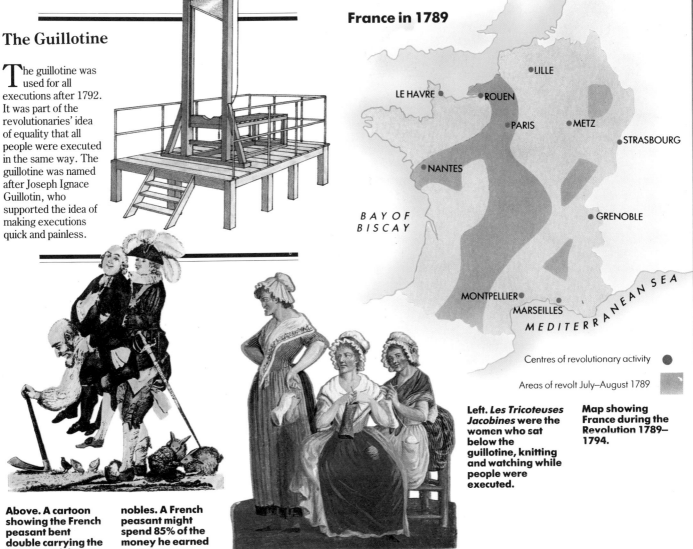

Centres of revolutionary activity ●

Areas of revolt July–August 1789 ▪

Left. *Les Tricoteuses Jacobines* were the women who sat below the guillotine, knitting and watching while people were executed.

Map showing France during the Revolution 1789–1794.

Above. A cartoon showing the French peasant bent double carrying the Church and the nobles. A French peasant might spend 85% of the money he earned on taxes.

paid no taxes at all, even though they were the ones who could afford to do so.

The thinkers of the Enlightenment (see pp. 30–31), like Rousseau, pointed to the unfairness of this. Such ideas of freedom fashioned the American Declaration of Independence (see p. 48) and altered the thinking of many middle-class people in France (who, like the peasants, also had to pay taxes). They were angry, too, that only the nobles could have the best jobs in the army, the navy and the government.

THE ESTATES GENERAL All these problems came to a head in 1789. French soldiers had fought for the Americans' freedom against the British in the War of Independence and had then returned to France, where the complete lack of freedom was obvious. Bad harvests in 1788 had led to widespread hunger and on top of this the king (Louis XVI, 1774–1792) had no money to pay the army, the navy, or the cost of running Versailles and running the country.

Louis decided to call the Estates General to ask them

to pay taxes. The Estates General, the nearest thing to *Parliament* in France, had not been called since 1614. It consisted of nobles, clergy and about 600 commoners (mostly middle-class merchants, bankers, lawyers and so on). For the first time, the king now asked the nobles and clergy to pay taxes. They were horrified.

Meanwhile, the commoners (known as the *Third Estate*) suggested that the payment of taxes to the king should allow them to have a say in the running of the country. The result was an uproar. Louis would not hear of such a thing. He locked the Estates General out of the hall they were meeting in at Versailles. They stormed out and met on the tennis court to discuss their complaints.

THE STORMING OF THE BASTILLE Matters went from bad to worse. On July 14, a mob of poor people stormed the *Bastille*, a royal fortress in Paris. To the Parisians it stood for all the power of the king, the nobles and the clergy. After the Bastille had fallen to the rioters, other riots followed all over France.

FRANCE: ROBESPIERRE TO NAPOLEON

In the summer of 1789 the Estates General re-formed itself as a National Assembly and got down to business, calling for a less powerful monarchy. Louis XVI would not agree, so he was arrested and brought to Paris. Time dragged on, but the king still would not agree to limiting his power. Finally, the mob stormed the palace of the Tuileries, where Louis was living, and fear of the mob helped persuade the National Assembly to put the king on trial and send him to the *guillotine* in 1793.

THE REPUBLIC Protests by moderate people were ignored. France was now ruled by a Committee of Public Safety and justice was carried out by a Revolutionary Tribunal. The extreme revolutionaries who wanted complete change were called *Jacobins*. (They even renamed the first year of the republic, 1792, as Year One.)

ROBESPIERRE (1758–1794) The Jacobins' leader was the pitiless Maximilien Robespierre, a clever lawyer and judge who had joined the Estates General at the age of 31 and who believed passionately in the rights of ordinary people. In Robespierre's view, it was only a rotten society and the work of evil men that stopped ordinary people from being perfect, so it was necessary to kill all the evil people.

Now the guillotine rose and fell day after day. The enemies of the people (at first only the rich) were destroyed one by one, starting with the widowed queen, Marie Antoinette, then the Duc of Orléans, then nobles and clergy. After this Robespierre hunted down the more moderate people who had previously supported him, like Danton, and their wives and families. Then he turned on rival Jacobins. Robespierre saw evil men and women everywhere.

To oppose the "Terror," as it was called, was a crime. For a year, all France lived in fear. About 500,000 people were arrested and 17,000 were guillotined. Finally, the frightened colleagues of Robespierre turned on him and he too was guillotined.

THE RISE OF NAPOLEON At first many people in Europe were pleased that the revolution was making the French more free. But other monarchs were alarmed because the French guillotined their monarch and nobles and declared they would support revolutions in other countries. By 1793, Austria, Prussia, Britain, Spain and the Netherlands were all at war with France.

Many of the army officers had fled from France to avoid the guillotine and the soldiers who were left were poorly equipped, although they were very loyal to France. An officer called Napoleon Bonaparte (1769–1821) took control. His first military success was at Toulon, where he defeated an army of rebel Frenchmen, the British and Spanish. From then on Napoleon seemed invincible.

THE DIRECTORY After the fall of Robespierre, the government was taken over by five men called the Directory. They supported Napoleon in his campaigns against the Austrians. In 1798, he set sail for Egypt to defeat the Turks and capture the British route to India. Although he did not succeed in this, Napoleon returned to France, overthrew the Directory and, with two others, became a consul of France. He became emperor in 1804.

The Jacobins

The Jacobins gained their name because they met in Paris in what used to be a Dominican (or Jacobin) convent. Their aim was to protect the gains of the French Revolution. They were the most powerful group in the government from mid-1793 to mid-1794, although many moderate people left the Club over the question of getting rid of the king.

There were probably about 500,000 members of Jacobin clubs at one time, but after the fall of their leader, Robespierre, the Jacobin clubs virtually closed down.

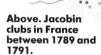

Above. Jacobin clubs in France between 1789 and 1791.

Right. Maximilien Robespierre.

Napoleon I (1769–1821)

Napoleon was born on the island of Corsica, which belonged to France. When he was 15 years old, he went to study at the military school in Paris. In 1793 he was in charge of the artillery at Toulon against the British and Spanish. He stormed the town and was made a general.

After that Napoleon fell out of favor and was so poor he had to sell his watch and books to survive. He was recalled in 1795, when he defended Paris against rebels and avoided civil war. He led the French army to defeat the Austrians and invade Egypt, and became First Consul of France in 1800. Later he became emperor.

Above. Map showing how large Napoleon's empire was and the places where his major battles took place. By 1812, he controlled most of western Europe.

Top. A painting showing the Battle of Aboukir Bay (Egypt) in 1798.

Right. Napoleon Bonaparte, painted by Jacques-Louis David. He is shown going forward to conquest.

The Eastern World
MANCHU CHINA

The wealth of China was based on farming. The fertile valleys of the Chang Jiang (Yangtze) and Huang He (Yellow) Rivers produced crops of rice, wheat and vegetables that fed China's vast population, which reached 100 million in 1650. However, one year in every five was reckoned to be a disaster, due either to drought or to flooding of the great river basins. Loss of the food crops led to starvation and often to rebellion.

THE MANCHUS In the seventeenth century, there were a number of food crises and rebellions in China. The Manchu people in the north saw their chance, surging southward, capturing the capital city of Beijing (Peking) and taking control of most of China by 1652.

The Manchus were not Chinese. In fact they never made up more than 2 percent of the population of China. They kept themselves separate and did not inter-marry with the Chinese. However, they took over all the Chinese ways of ruling, with the Manchu emperors using the enormous and efficient Chinese civil service to run the empire.

CHINESE SELF-SUFFICIENCY The Chinese always considered themselves at the center of the world, regarding those who lived beyond the boundaries of

Left. Map of China showing the major cities.

China as "barbarians." Although trade did exist (more at some periods of history than at others) between the west and China, the Chinese had never been very impressed with what the west could offer. In return for their beautiful silks, porcelain and *lacquerware*, all the Chinese wanted from the west was silver or gold. They had everything else that they wanted.

Since farming was considered the most important

Canton harbor, a busy Chinese port.

job, China was largely self-sufficient in food (able to grow enough to support its population). Barges loaded with rice, salt, sugar and tea sailed from south China, along the Grand Canal to Beijing. The rivers bustled with trade. China produced enough iron, silk, hemp, bamboo (used for pipes, tubes, bridges and so on), leather and wood for the needs of its farming people.

THE EUROPEANS As the eighteenth century wore on, it became more difficult for the Chinese to ignore the Europeans. The Emperor Ch'ien-lung (1735–1795) insisted that European traders should be allowed to call at only one port, Guangzhou (Canton). From there it was up to the Chinese to transport the goods to the emperor. Ch'ien-lung had his own view of these goods, looking on them as gifts from the European "barbarians." The Europeans, however, expected him to buy them. Moreover, they wanted to sell their goods all over China.

LORD MACARTNEY AND THE EMPEROR In 1792, the British sent Lord Macartney as the first ambassador to China. He took with him a hot air balloon; scientific instruments, such as telescopes, microscopes and sextants; clocks and watches, and air guns. The 83-year-old Emperor Ch'ien-lung was delighted. Macartney also presented a letter from King George III of Britain (1760–1820), asking the emperor for several things, including permission for British merchants to call at all Chinese ports. The emperor ignored the request.

Despite China's wish to remain separate from the rest of the world, the Europeans were becoming richer and more powerful. Within 50 years they were strong enough to force the Chinese to trade with them.

Emperor Kangxi (1661–1722)

Right. An embroidered court robe made of silk. Below. A decorated porcelain plate.

Above. These animal figures have been carved out of jade.

Kangxi became emperor at the age of seven. When he was 15 he took control. He defeated the three powerful warlords in the south of China before conquering Taiwan, parts of Russia, Outer Mongolia and Tibet.

He was also a great administrator, and set up projects to repair the Grand Canal and the flood control works on the Yellow River.

Kangxi loved studying. A European Jesuit missionary called Ferdinand Verbiest taught him geometry and became responsible for cannon production in China. The emperor's liking for the Jesuits encouraged other missionaries, but they were not tolerant of the Chinese. This led to all missionaries except the Jesuits being ordered to leave the country.

JAPAN DURING THE TOKUGAWA SHOGUNATE

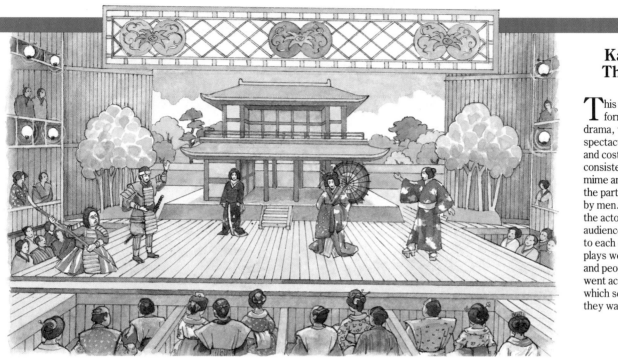

Kabuki Theater

This was a popular form of Japanese drama, with spectacular stage sets and costumes. It consisted of music, mime and dance. All the parts were played by men. Traditionally, the actors and audiences used to talk to each other. The plays went on all day and people came and went according to which scenes or plays they wanted to see.

By 1650, the Japanese, like the Chinese, had lost interest in the Europeans. They rejected both the European religion of Christianity and European trade.

TRADE In the seventeenth century, the only Europeans who were allowed to come to Japan were the Dutch. However, they could only send one ship a year, and they had to stay on the tiny island of Deshima in Nagasaki Harbor. The Japanese continued to trade with China and Korea, but the Japanese people themselves were forbidden by their government to travel abroad. (Death was the penalty for traveling abroad—if you were foolish enough to return!) To make sure that Japanese people stayed at home, the government forbade the building of any large ships. They felt threatened by the Europeans.

THE TOKUGAWA SHOGUNS All this could be done because the government in Japan was very strong. The emperor of Japan was simply a figurehead and the real power lay with the *shoguns*, the military leaders. In 1603, one family of shoguns, called the Tokugawa, had established its power over the others. From this time on there was only one shogun in Japan. All the others were now called *daimyos*. They ruled their own lands but they recognized the Tokugawa shogun as their leader. To make sure they were loyal, the shogun ordered them to

spend every other year at his capital, Edo (which is now Tokyo). There he could keep an eye on them and ensure that they did not become too powerful in their home lands.

This system of government lasted well into the nineteenth century. Japan prospered. Trade with China, Korea, the East Indies and Russia grew. Main roads were built to link all the big towns and ports of Japan.

SOCIETY Japanese society became more rigid, however. There were four levels: the most important men were warriors; next came craftsmen, then peasant farmers, and lastly merchants. No Japanese person could think of changing his or her level. The son of a peasant could not train as a craftsman. Even the warriors (*samurai*) could not change masters and go to serve another daimyo.

CONTROL By 1650, the penalty for being a Christian was death and so Christianity virtually disappeared from Japan. Then the Tokugawa shogun decided to get rid of guns, another European influence that had been brought to Japan in the sixteenth century. The daimyos had been fascinated by these guns. Not only did they buy them, their swordsmiths quickly learned how to make them. The Tokugawa shogun decided to turn the clock back.

He did not want the daimyos forming their own armies of samurai warriors armed with guns, so he granted fewer and fewer licences to gunsmiths until all the samurai were once more armed only with swords and had no guns at all.

Since Japan was peaceful during this period of history, there was very little for the samurai to do. Many started to work as administrators in the government rather than have nothing to do.

Japan seemed deliberately backward to the outside world, but in fact it was a well-organized, artistic and prosperous country. Three of the 10 biggest cities in the world in 1750 were in Japan. Tokyo was the largest Japanese city, with half a million inhabitants.

The picture above, painted by an anonymous Japanese artist, shows the execution of Jesuit priests in 1622. Christians were persecuted in Japan during the seventeenth century.

Right. The shogun, Tokugawa Ieyasu (1542–1616). He founded the dynasty of shoguns who ruled Japan from 1603 until 1868.

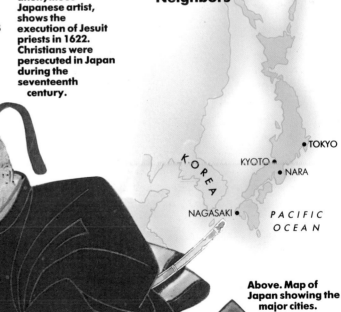

Japan and its Neighbors

TOKYO

KYOTO

NARA

KOREA

NAGASAKI

PACIFIC OCEAN

Above. Map of Japan showing the major cities.

MOGUL AND MARATHA INDIA

The *Mogul* emperors ruled a large part of India from the early sixteenth century to about 1750. Their religion was *Islam* and they were known as *Muslims*. The most famous Mogul emperor was Akbar, who reigned from 1556 to 1605. He brought about many reforms, such as the end of the enslavement of prisoners of war. More importantly for the future of India, he insisted on religious toleration. Prisoners of war and their women and children were not to be forced to become

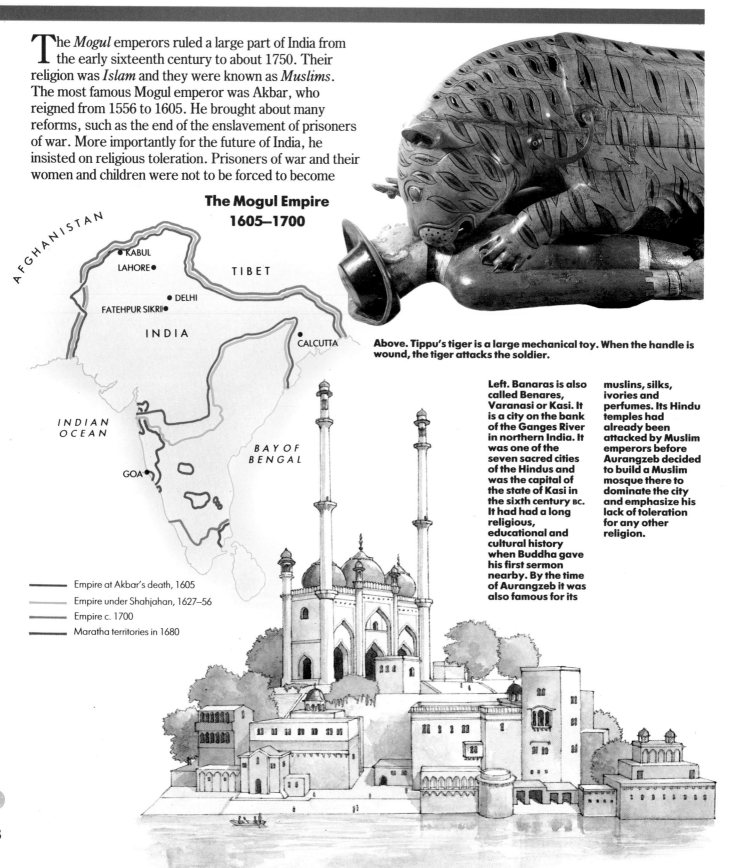

The Mogul Empire 1605–1700

AFGHANISTAN

● KABUL
LAHORE ●
TIBET
● DELHI
FATEHPUR SIKRI ●
INDIA
● CALCUTTA

INDIAN OCEAN

BAY OF BENGAL

GOA ●

——— Empire at Akbar's death, 1605
——— Empire under Shahjahan, 1627–56
——— Empire c. 1700
——— Maratha territories in 1680

Above. Tippu's tiger is a large mechanical toy. When the handle is wound, the tiger attacks the soldier.

Left. Banaras is also called Benares, Varanasi or Kasi. It is a city on the bank of the Ganges River in northern India. It was one of the seven sacred cities of the Hindus and was the capital of the state of Kasi in the sixth century BC. It had had a long religious, educational and cultural history when Buddha gave his first sermon nearby. By the time of Aurangzeb it was also famous for its muslins, silks, ivories and perfumes. Its Hindu temples had already been attacked by Muslim emperors before Aurangzeb decided to build a Muslim mosque there to dominate the city and emphasize his lack of toleration for any other religion.

Muslims. *Hindus* were not to be made to change their religion either. Akbar worked to make India into a united country with one official language but toleration for other languages and beliefs. He passed on a strong country to his successors, many of whom were clever rulers. However, they were frequently faced with rebellions, often led by their own sons, and this weakened the empire.

SIVAJI AND THE MARATHAS As the Mogul Empire weakened in the seventeenth century, another center of power arose further south. This was founded by Sivaji, leader of the *Marathas*, who wanted to conquer more land at about the same time that Emperor Aurangzeb (1658–1707) came to the Mogul throne.

The two men signed a treaty in 1665 in which Sivaji agreed to surrender to the Moguls 23 out of the 35 forts that he had conquered from another Indian prince. He also agreed to acknowledge the power of the Moguls. In return, Aurangzeb supported him in claiming many of the prince's lands.

Above. Aurangzeb, the Mogul emperor from 1658 to 1707. His name means "ornament of the throne."

When Sivaji visited Aurangzeb, he did not like the patronizing way he was treated at the Mogul court. He flew into a rage and fainted. Aurangzeb did not trust Sivaji, but he was afraid that Sivaji's followers might join with enemies of the Moguls and depose him. He put Sivaji under house arrest in comfortable surroundings. Sivaji, however, is reputed to have made his escape in a fruit basket.

Sivaji continued to fight and conquer other lands. He built up a strong army and, seeing trouble from Europe, developed a navy as well.

THE ATTRACTION OF INDIA The Europeans were attracted by the wealth of India. Its main exports were precious stones (including diamonds, rubies, sapphires and pearls), cotton textiles (such as calico), sugar, pepper, ivory and a dye called indigo. The Europeans were fascinated by such exotic riches. The Portuguese already had small trading stations on the coast of India, and they were now followed by the Dutch and the British.

Above. An East India Company trading station in Bengal, 1665. These stations, often called factories, were big warehouses and were built like fortresses. European traders and their families lived inside them.

CLIVE OF INDIA

Robert Clive

Clive went to India as a clerk in the East India Company, but soon became a soldier. He went on to lead British troops to defeat Indian and French forces and establish British rule in India.

In the picture on the left, Emperor Sha Alam hands Clive an edict that gives the Company the right to collect revenues from Bengal, Bihar and Orissa.

Clive returned to Britain in 1767. His rule in India had made him unpopular and he killed himself in 1774.

Both Britain and France, together with other European powers, had started to set up trading stations in India from the middle of the seventeenth century. As in other parts of the world during this period, the British and the French were strong rivals in trade.

The chance for France to gain the upper hand over the British in India came in 1748. Two princes of Indian states claimed a strip of land called the Carnatic, on the east coast of India, where the French and the British both had trading stations. The French supported one prince, called Chanda. The British supported the other, Mohammed Ali.

ROBERT CLIVE (1725–1774) The British trading activities in India at this time were run by the British East India Company, which sent an army of 500 men to help Mohammed Ali. This army, led by Robert Clive, captured Carnatic and then held out for 53 days when it was besieged by an army 20 times larger. The fighting dragged on, but eventually Mohammed Ali was made ruler of the area. He favored the British, who gained more trade through his friendship.

THE BLACK HOLE OF CALCUTTA, 1756 Both the French and the British had trading stations in Bengal, the state ruled by Suraj-ud-Daulah, who favored the French. In a dispute with the British over an enemy of Suraj's whom they were sheltering, he attacked the British trading station of Fort William. After a fight, 145 British survivors surrendered. Suraj locked them in a cell measuring six by five meters. Without water and with only two, small, barred windows, the prisoners struggled for air through the hot tropical night. When the door was opened in the morning, 123 people had died of suffocation or had been trampled to death. This incident made the British furious.

THE BATTLE OF PLASSEY, 1757 Clive, with an army of 3000, pursued Suraj. Camping overnight at the village of Plassey, they awoke in the morning to face a semi-circle of 60,000 of Suraj's soldiers. However, with the help of an

Left. Mohammed Ali, the Indian prince whom the British supported.

Indian Arts and Crafts

Mogul India was famous for carpets, glassware and paintings. The carpets were made of fine wool that was often mistaken for silk. Glassware was made by craftsmen who painted designs onto colored glass.

Many paintings were done for book illustrations, showing birds and animals, court scenes and stories from history.

Left. An official of the British East India Company living in great style and splendor in India. Notice the English portraits but the Indian furnishings.

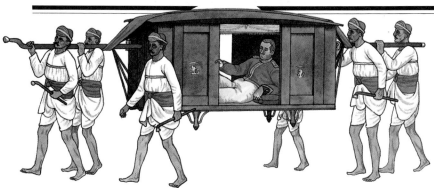

Left. An official of the Company being carried in a litter by Indian servants.

1 In 1760, China reached its greatest size under the Ch'ing dynasty. It took in Manchuria, Mongolia, Tibet, Korea, Taiwan and Eastern Turkestan as well as Inner China.

2 In 1762, Jean-Jacques Rousseau of France, one of the leading figures of the Enlightenment, wrote *The Social Contract*. This said that governments should act for the good of the people they governed and should give them justice and equality.

3 In 1768, James Cook of Britain began his exploration of the Pacific Ocean, coming across many places, including New Zealand and Australia, that Europeans had known little or nothing about before.

4 In 1776, the 13 colonies in North America declared their independence from Britain. This was the beginning of the end of Britain's first empire.

5 In 1789, revolution broke out in France. This led to the execution of King Louis XVI and the setting up of a revolutionary government which was eventually taken over by Napoleon Bonaparte.

Indian general, Mir Jaffir, who had deserted from Suraj, Clive's army won the Battle of Plassey.

THE IMPORTANCE OF PLASSEY TO THE BRITISH The Battle of Plassey gained an area of land for Britain the size of England and Wales. Mir Jaffir was made ruler of all Bengal, but the British had the real power. From then until the mid-twentieth century, the British were dominant in India.

Up to 1750 the economic effects of the British in India were small, However, once they gained control of Bengal after the Battle of Plassey, they became much more powerful. Some British merchants made huge fortunes and many came back to Britain to spend them. They were known as *nabobs*. People like Clive, and later Warren Hastings, tried to reform the British East India Company and the British government had some control over it after the India Act of 1784. Despite this, the British in India were still making fortunes in the early part of the nineteenth century. Although some Europeans went to India as *missionaries* or to work as administrators, it was trade and the money to be made from it that were the most important reasons why the British, like other Europeans, were interested in India at this time.

The Growth of British Power in India

■ British possessions in India to 1805

Above. Map showing India in the eighteenth century and the growth of British power up to 1805. The areas they controlled were in the south, along the east coast and on the northern border. The Marathas were the only rival to British power by 1805.

61

Africa
AFRICA AND THE SLAVE TRADE

The Slaves

In the late 1500s, a few thousand slaves were transported from Africa to the New World every year. The figure peaked (50,000–100,000 a year) in the eighteenth century.

Altogether, 10 million slaves were recorded as landing alive in the New World, with two million dying during the voyages. The real figures for deaths may have been much higher.

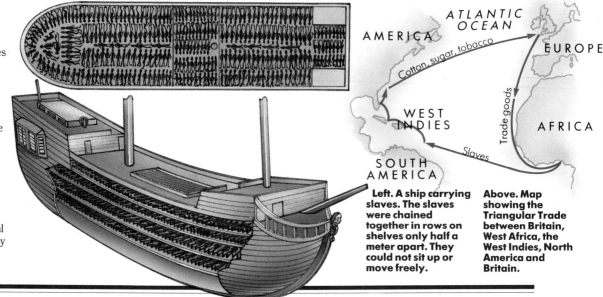

Left. A ship carrying slaves. The slaves were chained together in rows on shelves only half a meter apart. They could not sit up or move freely.

Above. Map showing the Triangular Trade between Britain, West Africa, the West Indies, North America and Britain.

For centuries most of North Africa was dominated by Arabs, who traded with the Mediterranean countries to the north as well as with kingdoms such as Ghana and Mali in West Africa, south of the Sahara Desert. The trade was in goods like copper, horses and salt from the north, and in ivory, gold and slaves from the West African kingdoms.

Most people in East Africa were farmers. They had little to do with the people on the coast, where a great deal of trade had taken place for centuries. Trading centered on coastal towns like Mombasa (now in Kenya), which had a population of about 10,000 by 1500. Many of the traders were Arabs, or of mixed Arab and African descent, and trading ships went as far afield as China.

The huge areas in the center of Africa were largely untouched by Europeans until after 1800. However, the growth of the slave trade greatly affected the people who lived on the coast, as well as many people who lived inland and were captured and sold as slaves. Slavery was not new to places like West Africa. The kings of that area had sold captured prisoners into slavery for centuries.

THE EUROPEANS Parts of North Africa, trading stations down the coasts of West and East Africa, and the Dutch settlement in South Africa were the only footholds that the Europeans had in Africa by 1800. Yet Europeans

Slave Trade Routes

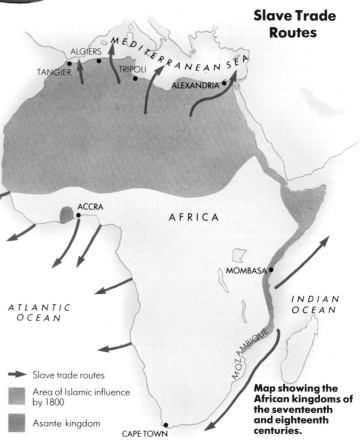

→ Slave trade routes

░ Area of Islamic influence by 1800

▓ Asante kingdom

Map showing the African kingdoms of the seventeenth and eighteenth centuries.

The Kingdom of Asante

In the 1670s Osei Tutu founded the kingdom of Asante as a loose confederation. Chiefs paid him tribute taxes collected from their villages and the profits from their gold fields. They provided soldiers for a confederation army led by Osei Tutu.

By 1750 the Asante controlled most of the gold fields and most of modern Ghana. This made the Asante kings very wealthy.

Most of the gold mines were worked by slave labor. The gold was used to buy cloth, metal, European firearms and salt from the many traders who passed through the area.

Above. This comb was used as part of a burial ritual. When it was found, it had a crust of lime, egg and millet on it. These were the foods given to the spirits.

Left. A mask representing the head of an enemy. It was probably attached to a stool.

Above. Breast ornament of the Asantehene, or king of the Asante. Other ornaments included bracelets, headbands and necklaces made of finely worked gold. The king's base or capital was near Kumasi, a great trading center.

THE TRIANGULAR TRADE By 1650, the British and French had joined the Dutch in the slave trade. Merchants loaded ships with cotton cloth, beads, alcohol and cheap guns and sailed to Africa, where they traded these goods for young black men and women. Then they set sail for the Americas. In America, the slaves were traded (for two or three times the price paid for them) for items like sugar, rum, raw cotton, coffee and tobacco. The merchants then sailed back to Europe to sell these goods, having made a good profit.

were already affecting the future of the continent by taking people from there to work on the new plantations and in the mines of the Americas. This was slavery on a greater scale than Africa had ever known.

Sugar cane plantations were set up in the West Indies and were followed by cotton and tobacco plantations in the southern part of North America, and by sugar and coffee plantations in Brazil. All these plantations needed large numbers of people to work them. The native Amerindians were almost wiped out by European disease and violence. European slaves (mostly convicts) were too few in number and quickly died of tropical disease. So the Europeans turned to Africa for slaves.

THE SLAVES During this period of history, there were many wars between different African tribes. The tribe that had won often sold the prisoners it had taken to dealers. These dealers in turn sold the slaves to European traders, who chained and packed them naked into special slave ships for the journey to America. Up to a third died on each voyage, and were thrown overboard.

Once in the Americas, the Africans were sold as livestock. Some never recovered from the trauma of their capture and voyage. With no hope of seeing their home again, a third of the slaves died within three years of their arrival. Few of the rest survived the hard labor on the plantations for more than 10 years.

63

THE DUTCH AND SOUTH AFRICA

The Dutch governor of the Cape Colony in South Africa on his farm. Compare the architecture of the house with the Dutch houses on page 20.

The area of land that came to be known as South Africa was not an empty land when the Dutch first landed there in the seventeenth century. There were many different tribes and peoples living there, including hunter-gatherer societies and tribes which farmed cattle and sheep. These tribes traded among themselves. For instance, the *Khoisan* obtained their copper and iron from the *Batswana* to the north of them, trading the metals that they did not use with the *Xhosa* in exchange for tobacco. Trade spread right across the region.

The most important group as far as the white settlers were concerned was the Khoisan. About 50,000 of these cattle and sheep farmers lived in the south of Africa in the seventeenth century.

CAPE TOWN The first Dutch sailors who landed in South Africa were on their way to the Dutch colonies in the East Indies. They needed fresh meat, vegetables and water, because they were only part of the way through this long voyage, and they bought these goods from the Khoisan. As more and more Dutch ships stopped at the Cape, the sailors wanted more and more food. If they could not persuade the Khoisan to sell to them, they sometimes seized their animals. Then the Dutch decided it would be easier to set up their own farms around Cape Town, so that they could grow their own food to supply their sailors.

SETTLEMENT Dutch people came out to South Africa to settle on farms within 100 kilometers of Cape Town. They grew wheat and fruit and became known as Boers (*boer* is the Dutch word for farmer). In 1685, French Protestants, known as Huguenots, began to be persecuted in France by Louis XIV (see p. 22) and some came to settle in South Africa. They were expert wine-makers and were soon growing vines and farming.

LABOR Slavery was introduced in 1658. The Boers found that the local tribes were too independent to work on the Dutch farms, preferring to follow their own ways of life. So the Dutch brought in slaves from places such as West Africa and Malaysia.

ISOLATION AND RELIGION As the population of European settlers grew and all the land around Cape Town was settled, the Boers trekked northeast to found new farms. The climate here was drier, so they raised sheep and cattle instead of growing wheat and fruit.

The Boers lived on huge farms, cut off from the civilized life of Cape Town. They developed their own language, called Afrikaans, which was a simpler form of Dutch and included many African words.

The settlers had brought with them a very strict form of Christianity, called *Calvinism*, and they found justification for owning slaves in the Old Testament. In practical terms, it seemed the only way to run the big farms they had.

The further the Dutch spread out from Cape Town, the more they threatened the ways of life of the native peoples of southern Africa. Clashes between the Boers, the Khoisan and different *Bantu* people started before 1800, but the real trouble came later. The hunter-gatherers were either pushed further away from the fertile land, into areas like the Kalahari Desert, or they had to work for the Boers.

The Khoisan and the Dutch

In the mid-seventeenth century, about 50,000 members of the Khoisan tribes lived in the area behind what became Cape Town. At first they welcomed trade with the Dutch, but as more and more white people came their land was threatened. Arguments led to the first Khoi-Dutch war in 1659. Although the Khoisan tribes united and drove back the Dutch, they could not capture the Dutch fort and eventually had to give up.

Afterwards there was a meeting of Khoisan and Dutch leaders. A Dutchman called Van Riebeeck recorded in his diary:

They spoke for a long time about our taking every day more of the land which had

Above. Khoisan people trading with Dutch sailors.

belonged to them from all ages. They also asked whether, if they were to come to Holland, they would be permitted to act in a

similar manner.

At the end of the meeting, the Dutch leaders said that the Khoisan had lost their land in war, and

therefore could not expect to get it back.

From this time on the Khoisan were in retreat. They had three choices: to fight

the Dutch, to move further north, or to become servants of the Dutch farmers.

1 In North Africa, which included Algeria and Egypt, the Ottoman Turks had established an empire by 1500. Arab influence in North Africa remained very strong and throughout the period 1650 to 1800 it extended southwards, through trade in items such as gold and slaves.

2 In West Africa, the sixteenth century had seen the rise of the highly developed states of Benin and Oyo. By the eighteenth century, the more powerful states were Dahomey and Asante on the Gold Coast.

3 In East Africa, Arab influence extended down the coast almost to South Africa. In the interior, however, Ethiopia and other states continued to control their own affairs.

4 Central Africa was largely untouched by outside influences by 1800. Tribes here lived off the land, trading some goods, such as copper, when required.

5 The Russian tsar, Peter the Great, began to build the city of St. Petersburg in 1703. It became the capital of Russia.

6 Dutch settlers in the East Indies began growing coffee there in 1711. Soon there were large coffee plantations and by 1723 about 13 million pounds were being produced each year.

Dutch Expansion in South Africa

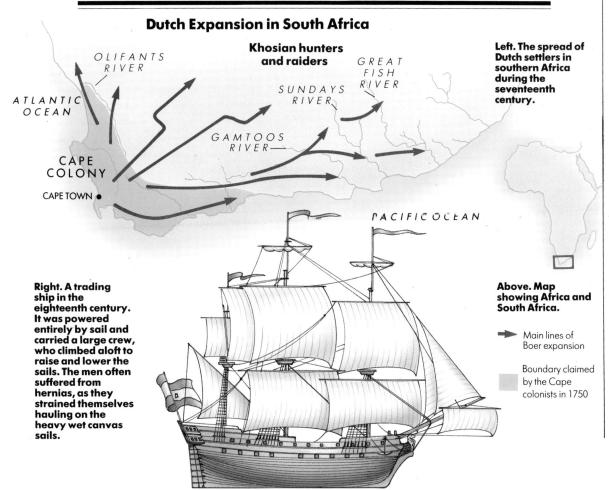

OLIFANTS RIVER

Khosian hunters and raiders

GREAT FISH RIVER

SUNDAYS RIVER

ATLANTIC OCEAN

GAMTOOS RIVER

CAPE COLONY

CAPE TOWN •

Left. The spread of Dutch settlers in southern Africa during the seventeenth century.

PACIFIC OCEAN

Above. Map showing Africa and South Africa.

→ Main lines of Boer expansion

Boundary claimed by the Cape colonists in 1750

Right. A trading ship in the eighteenth century. It was powered entirely by sail and carried a large crew, who climbed aloft to raise and lower the sails. The men often suffered from hernias, as they strained themselves hauling on the heavy wet canvas sails.

65

Exploring the Fringes of the World
ABORIGINAL AUSTRALIANS

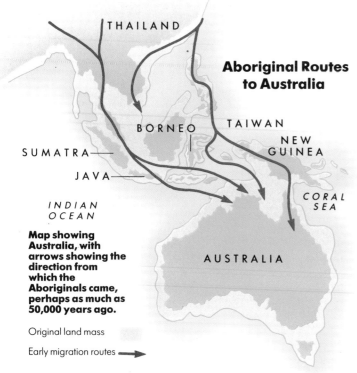

Aboriginal Routes to Australia

THAILAND

BORNEO

TAIWAN

NEW GUINEA

SUMATRA

JAVA

INDIAN OCEAN

CORAL SEA

AUSTRALIA

Map showing Australia, with arrows showing the direction from which the Aboriginals came, perhaps as much as 50,000 years ago.

Original land mass

Early migration routes ➝

The first people to live in Australia came from Asia, possibly as much as 50,000 years ago. They probably journeyed from one island to the next in canoes or rafts. These people were the discoverers and colonizers of Australia.

HUNTER-GATHERERS At the point in history at which people settled in Australia, all the people on earth were nomadic hunter-gatherers. As time wore on, most people changed from living as nomads to being settled farmers. However, this did not happen in Australia because of the general lack of water and resources throughout the land. Thus, most Aboriginals continued as nomads and had to live in balance with the food and water available during each season. Groups of men, women and children adapted to what was available in each area, whether the land was rich or arid. People lived in small groups throughout Australia. They differed from each other in their physical appearance, language, beliefs, traditions and cultures.

TRADE AND RELIGION About 3000 years ago, some Aboriginal tribes began to travel long distances to trade ornaments and other goods with other tribes. In areas that were better for farming, such as the swamp regions of inland Victoria, there were settled villages where as many as 700 people lived.

Ritual life was extremely important to the Aboriginals. Ceremonial gatherings took place on sacred sites, such as the painted rock shelters associated with the idea of *dreamtime*, which is a mythical golden age of the past. Hundreds of people came from miles away to gather for short periods at such occasions. These ceremonies were often associated with the harvest of special foods, such as the *cycad nut* or the *bogong moth*.

By the time that Europeans arrived in Australia, the Aboriginals had successfully adapted to the often difficult environment of their country. They ate many different kinds of plant and animal food, from the *witchetty grub* to the kangaroo, from oysters to flying foxes, and from turtle eggs to the roots of daisy yams.

THE COMING OF THE EUROPEANS Australia was first sighted by a European—the Dutch explorer Willem Janszoon—in 1605. Abel Tasman, another Dutchman,

Fighting between the British and Aboriginals in the early nineteenth century.

Above. An Aboriginal bark painting of a kangaroo.

Above. *Uluru* (Ayers Rock) was and is a sacred place to Aboriginals.

Left. An Aboriginal picture of the "lightning man," Obiri Rock.

The Aboriginal Dreamtime

In Aboriginal belief, long ago the world was only a flat emptiness. Then the Ancestors or Beings came out of the earth and made the hills and valleys, the rivers, lakes, springs, trees, plants and animals. The Aboriginals' name for this time of creation is the Dreamtime.

When they had finished their work of creating the world, the Ancestors sank back into the earth, but their spirit is still in the world—in the rocks and trees and all around.

Usually the Ancestors were in human form, but they could take the shapes of animals if they wished to. The Aboriginals give the Ancestors many names, some of which mean "dream."

Each of the many Aboriginal tribal groups had (and still has) sacred places. *Uluru* (Ayers Rock) in the middle of Australia is the sacred place of two groups of the Pitjantjara tribe. These sacred places are where the Ancestors lived, hunted and performed ceremonies to show the way that the Aboriginals are to live their lives. There are many pictures at the sacred places that illustrate the doings of the Ancestors.

sighted Tasmania in 1642 and sailed right along the northern and part of the western coasts of Australia in 1644. However, Australia remained undisturbed until the British Admiralty sent Captain James Cook to explore the continent. He claimed it for the British in 1770. From 1788 Britain sent convicts to serve their prison sentences in Australia. Many of them stayed on in the country when their sentences were over. Other settlers gradually began to arrive too.

Soon after the European arrival, the number of Aboriginals fell sharply. It has been estimated that there were 300,000 Aboriginals in 1770; by 1900, the population amounted to about 66,000. Many died from bullets and many more from the strange European diseases, such as tuberculosis. The rest had lost their land and their sacred places. It was not their home any longer. The Aboriginals became despondent and the death rate rose dramatically. The European colonists, however, grew rich and their numbers increased.

Left. The Aboriginals built shelters out of whatever materials were available. Often these were wood, twigs and leaves. Shelters could be semi-permanent, depending on how much a tribe moved around in search of food. More permanent villages were built in areas that were rich in food supplies, like the swamp regions of inland Victoria.

MAORI NEW ZEALAND

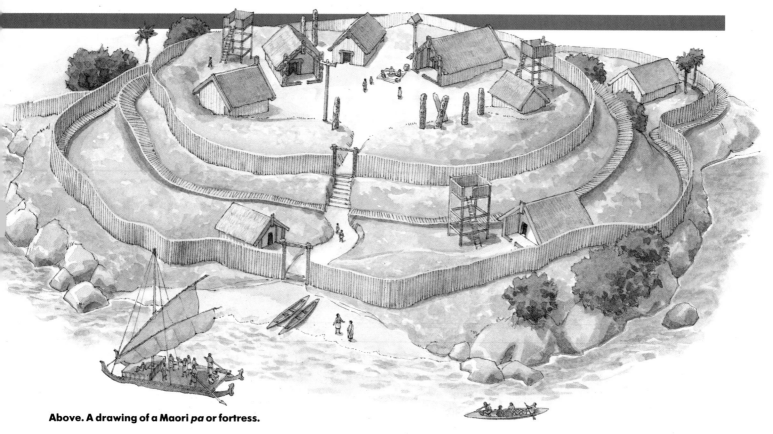

Above. A drawing of a Maori *pa* or fortress.

People from Polynesia sailed to New Zealand around AD 1350. They were already farmers and settled down to grow yams, sweet potatoes and taro on North Island. However, the colder climate of South Island made farming impossible there, so on that island small groups of nomads lived by fishing and gathering native plants. The people who settled in New Zealand were called Maoris.

THE MOAS Over time, the number of people in the warmer northern regions of North Island grew quite large. They hunted flightless birds, called *moas*, which were easy prey. The moa was extremely important to the Maoris. It was a large bird, possibly bigger than an ostrich. Its flesh was used for food, its bones were carved into tools and ornaments, and the shells of its enormous eggs were used as containers for carrying water. As time passed, however, the moa became extinct and the Maoris became more dependent on farming.

MAORI WARFARE As tribes grew larger, they needed more land to grow food, and fights over land became

Tattooing

The way in which the Maoris tattooed themselves was more like carving. They used tiny chisels to carve intricate patterns into the skin. It was very painful. Men had more tattooing on their faces than women did. Tattooing was done all over the body, sometimes including the thighs and buttocks as well.

There is no-one alive today tattooed in this way. The last man tattooed like this died 50 years ago, but there are still a few old people with tattooing on parts of their faces.

Maori Defended Settlements

- Defended settlement, or 'pa'

PAERA PA

RUARANGI PA

RAHAPARA PA

WHARETAEWA PA

TANIWHA PA

TASMAN SEA

NORTH ISLAND

SOUTH PACIFIC OCEAN

PACIFIC OCEAN

TARATA PA

SOUTH ISLAND

Right. A map of New Zealand showing where *pa* were built. Most settlements were around the coast and more people settled in North Island, where the climate was better for farming.

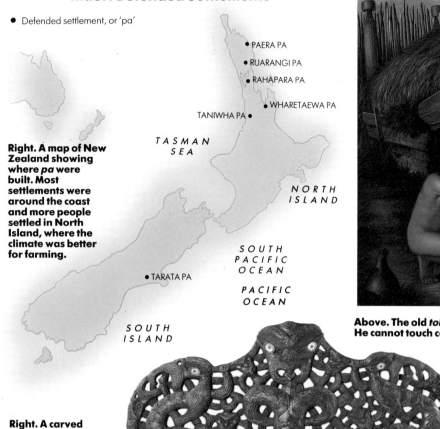

Above. The old *tohunga*, or wise man, is in a *tapu*, or sacred state. He cannot touch cooked food, so the boy is feeding him.

Right. A carved lintel showing the skill and detail of Maori work. Compare this style with the picture of the face on the page opposite.

Right. The moa was an enormous bird which could not fly. It was related to the ostrich but was much larger; some were three meters (compare the size of the chicken next to it). Once the Maoris arrived and started to hunt them, moas quickly became extinct.

common. The Maoris built fortresses, called *pa*, with terraces, ditches and palisades, on the sides of extinct volcanoes, on fairly flat land and even on swampy ground. As time went on, tribes of Maoris built more and more large *pa* and their defenses became stronger. Accounts from the eighteenth century describe houses and storehouses around central open spaces, called *marae*, and sometimes even plots of land on which to grow vegetables inside the walls of the fortresses.

The men taught Maori martial arts to the boys from an early age. Their weapons were designed for hand-to-hand fighting and were used for stabbing, thrusting or clubbing. War was usually caused by arguments over land and property, but the honor (*mana*) of the tribe also had to be guarded against insults of all kinds and any such insults were avenged. Feuds could continue for generations. There were also periods of peace when enemy tribes might join forces to fight a third enemy.

RELIGION OF THE MAORIS Religion was an important part of daily life; an important belief was *tapu*. This means "sacred" or "forbidden"—the same as the word "taboo." Certain places, objects, activities or even

people might be *tapu*. They had to be avoided altogether or treated with great care, under the direction of a *tohunga*—a sort of priest or wiseman. Otherwise, the Maoris believed that terrible misfortunes would happen to them. Though this may seem superstitious, this religious attitude to life also acted as a way of making sure that people behaved well. If someone failed to observe a *tapu* restriction, the *tohunga* soon made sure that they were punished in some way.

THE COMING OF THE EUROPEANS A Dutchman, named Abel Tasman, visited New Zealand in 1642, but it was not until the arrival of Captain James Cook in 1769 that real contact was made with the Europeans. Along with materials, such as iron, cloth and pottery, that the Maoris thought were wonderful, the Europeans also brought diseases which the Maoris had never known and to which they had no natural immunity.

The first Europeans to live in New Zealand were a rough crowd—escaped convicts from Australia, seamen from visiting whaling and trading ships, and a few adventurers. Many of the Maori died and their way of life changed forever.

THE UNTOUCHED WORLD

The Arctic World

ARCTIC OCEAN

ALASKA

NORTH AMERICA

ATLANTIC OCEAN

PACIFIC OCEAN

SOUTH AMERICA

Arctic settlement

ARCTIC OCEAN

LAPPLAND

EUROPE

ASIA

PACIFIC OCEAN

AFRICA

Above. Map showing the areas where the Inuit and Saami lived.

Captain John Ross meeting Inuit people in the early nineteenth century. This is the first recorded meeting of white people with Inuit.

By 1800, almost every part of the world had been touched by the arrival of the Europeans. The voyages of exploration and discovery from the late fifteenth century to the seventeenth century had uncovered whole new worlds for the Europeans. The cultures of the South and North American Indians, various African tribes, the Aboriginals of Australia and the Maoris of New Zealand had been revealed in exotic places which must have been beyond many Europeans' imaginations.

TRADE AT ANY COST At this time in history, Europeans embarked on voyages of exploration in order to increase their trading opportunities. When they arrived in "new" lands, their main interest was to find out what goods these lands could provide to be shipped back to Europe. The Europeans strengthened their claim on a new trading post by colonizing it. In this process, little thought was given to, or interest shown in, the cultures that they came across, and almost every such culture suffered through contact with the Europeans. The rapid depletion in numbers of all *indigenous* cultures was a great price to pay for European expansion.

THE ARCTIC WORLD The only cultures to remain untouched during this process were those of the Saami and Inuit (Eskimos) of the Arctic. From c. 10,000 BC, people who seem to have originated in central Asia migrated across the Bering land bridge into Arctic America. These were the ancestors of the Inuit. A similar development took place in Europe, where hunting groups moved from the east, south and west into Lappland—an area that covers northern Norway, Sweden, Finland and the Kola peninsula of Russia. The Inuit of America and the Saami of Lappland were separate groups, but there were many similarities in their cultures.

Inuit Dwellings

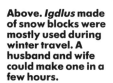

The polar Inuit people spent the winter in houses called *igdlus*. The shape of the *igdlu* and the sleeping platform inside it were cut into the ground. The walls and roof were made of rock slabs. The top of the roof was turfed and a window made of seal-gut was put in.

Blubber lamps inside gave heat and light and made it so warm that people did not need to wear many clothes.

There was not much space. The men mended tools and sledges. The women made clothes from animal skins. Everyone in the family slept on a sleeping platform covered with rugs.

Above. *Igdlus* made of snow blocks were mostly used during winter travel. A husband and wife could make one in a few hours.

Right. *Igdlus* of a more permanent kind were made from rock slabs dug in to the earth. They were covered with turf to insulate them against the freezing temperatures.

THE SAAMI The Saami lived by hunting, fowling and fishing. Elk and bear were frequently hunted and later reindeer were herded and used to pull sledges.

Shamanism was the main Saami religion and in this religion the bear was regarded as sacred. The Saami had a cult in which the animal was killed, the meat was eaten and the bones were buried with the skull at the top. Animal sacrifices were also carried out next to unusual trees and stones.

Inuit Religion

Shamanism is important in the religious life of the Inuits. A "shaman" is a person in the tribe who can heal the sick and communicate with the spirits. Often he is chosen because he is different from other people—he might have more teeth or an extra finger. The shaman frequently has the ability to go into a state of ecstasy.

Very often the shaman is not only a healer and central figure of ceremonies but is much respected and may become a leader.

Below. An Inuit mask representing the spirit of the Moon.

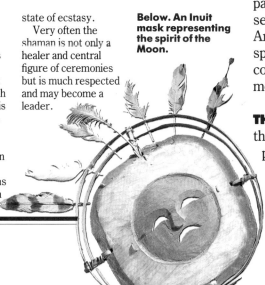

From the sixteenth century onwards, the Saami used portable tents, known as *Kåta*, to live in. The *Kåta* was divided into two sections: the sleeping area at the front, and the sacred kitchen and hearth at the back.

THE INUIT The early Inuit usually lived in flimsy hide tents. By the time of the Dorset culture (AD 800–1000), however, their settlements had grown larger. They built houses which were partly underground and which could hold up to three families each.

A later culture, the Thule of Alaska (AD 1000–1600), had a successful economy in which whaling played a large part. They used dog sledges, boats and kayaks and had a settled lifestyle with well-insulated winter homes. Around AD 1100, the Thule expanded eastwards and spread over a territory ranging from the east Siberian coast to Greenland. They were the ancestors of the modern-day Inuit (Eskimo).

THE EUROPEANS The first European to come across the Inuit was a British man, Captain John Ross. He met a party of Thule Inuit in 1818 when he was leading an expedition searching for a northwest passage to India and the East. European expansion had reached the last untouched culture and was soon to have a devastating effect on the lifestyle of the Inuit.

Revolution and Empire
TIME CHART

	CHINA AND JAPAN	THE AMERICAS	INDIA	AFRICA AND AUSTRALASIA
AD				
1652				Foundation of Cape Colony by the Dutch in South Africa
1653			The Taj Mahal in Agra is completed	
1658			Aurangzeb ascends the throne of the Mogul Empire	
1659				The French found a trading station on the Senegal coast
1662				Destruction of the Kongo Kingdom by the Portuguese
1664		New Amsterdam (New York) taken by the British	French East India Company is founded	
1674			Sivaji creates the Hindu Maratha Kingdom	
1688>1703	The regime of the Tokugawa shoguns in Japan reaches a peak			
1690			Foundation of Calcutta by the English	
1693		Gold discovered in Brazil		
1697	Chinese occupy Outer Mongolia			
1699>1702		Start of French colonization of Louisiana		
1700			The Punjab becomes a Sikh state	Creation of the Dyula Kingdom of Kong (Ivory Coast) Rise of Ashanti power on the Gold Coast (Ghana) of West Africa
1707			Death of Aurangzeb. Mogul Empire begins to decline	
1716>1751	Reign of the Japanese shogun Tokugawa Yoshimune.			
1730				Revival of the Borno Empire of Central Sudan
1731	Chinese occupy Tibet			
1736>1799	The reign of Ch'ing Emperor Ch'ien-lung			
1756>1763		Seven Years' War between the French and British		
1757			Battle of Plassey Robert Clive defeats the Indian troops of the Nawab of Bengal	
1761			Capture of Pondicherry. British destroy French power in India	
1764>1765		American colonists protest over British-imposed stamp duties		
1770				Captain James Cook claims Australia for Britain
1773		The Boston Tea Party		
1775	China's population is 264 million			
1775>1783		American War of Independence		
1776		The Declaration of Independence		
1788				Foundation of New South Wales in Australia as a convict settlement
1789		George Washington becomes the first US president		

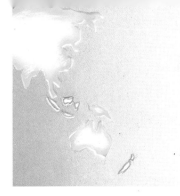 

GLOSSARY

absolute ruler A leader who has complete power. He or she makes all the laws and every decision about governing the country.

alchemy An early form of chemistry, chiefly concerned with finding a way to change ordinary metals into gold.

Amerindians The original inhabitants of the American continents.

Bantu An African tribe. The word is also used to mean all the original peoples of southern Africa.

Bastille The fortress and prison in Paris at the time of the French Revolution. For ordinary people, it symbolized the harsh way they were treated by their monarchs and the nobility.

Batswana A tribe of African people.

bogong moth An edible Australian moth.

botany The study of plants.

Calvinism The beliefs of a group of Protestants who follow the ideas of John Calvin.

cavalry The part of an army that is made up of soldiers on horseback.

censorship Limits put on the freedom for people to write (and read) whatever they like in books and newspapers.

couchée The ceremony of the French king going to bed. He was attended by a large number of courtiers, some of whom had the job of undressing him.

crop rotation A system of farming where a different crop is grown in the same field each year. This is because each crop takes different minerals out of the soil, so changing them round allows the soil to recover these minerals.

cycad nut An edible Australian nut.

fallow Leaving a field free of crops (usually for a year), to let the soil rest.

feudalism A way of organizing medieval society, stretching from the monarch to the nobility and down to people with no power at all. The people at the top granted land to those below, in return for military or labor services.

First Estate The nobility. This term is used particularly to refer to the French nobility.

guillotine An instrument that was used in France to behead people found guilty of certain crimes. During the French Revolution it was used to behead the king and queen, and many other people.

herders People who live by herding animals.

Hindus Followers of the ancient Eastern religion of Hinduism.

Huguenots French Protestants.

hunter-gatherers People who live by hunting and gathering food.

indigenous The original inhabitants, animals and plants of a country.

inflation Increasing prices.

Islam The Muslim religion founded by Muhammad.

Jacobins A powerful political party in France at the time of the Revolution.

janissaries Well-trained soldiers, originally slaves from Christian families, who fought in the army of the Muslim Turkish sultan.

Khoisan A tribe of people in southern Africa.

lacquerware Ornamental goods from the East that became popular in the West in the eighteenth century. They were covered in a coating of lacquer made from the lac tree.

levée The ceremony of the French king getting up in the morning. He was attended by a large number of courtiers, some of whom had the job of dressing him.

Marathas The Hindu rulers of western India in the Middle Ages.

marriage market A term used to describe how wealthy parents looked for husbands or wives for their children. It was called a "market" because this was done in a businesslike way, choosing the best partner from all those available.

militia Men who are signed up as soldiers to defend their local area.

missionaries People who work to convert others to their religion.

moas Giant birds of New Zealand, now extinct.

Moguls The Islamic rulers of India from 1526 to 1707.

Mule A machine for spinning cotton, invented by Samuel Crompton in 1779.

musketeer A soldier armed with a gun called a musket.

Muslims Followers of the religion of Islam.

nabobs British merchants who made their fortunes in India.

nation states Countries that rule themselves.

New World The Americas.

noble savage A term used during the Enlightenment to describe native peoples, who were thought to be honest and unspoilt by "civilization."

nomadic A term used to describe people who do not live in one place, but move from one area to another.

pa A Maori fortress.

Parliament An assembly of people who have been elected to govern a country. They meet to discuss matters such as new laws, the spending of taxes and whether to go to war.

philosophers People who are interested in knowledge and study ideas about how people should live.

pike-man A soldier armed with a pike, a weapon rather like a spear.

Pilgrim Fathers The settlers who sailed from England to America in 1620.

plague An epidemic disease. During the seventeenth century the term usually referred to the bubonic plague.

prism A triangular shape of glass used to split white light up into seven separate colours.

Puritans Protestants who have very strict beliefs and simple ("pure") church services.

Quakers Members of a religious group founded by George Fox (1624–1691).

reclaiming land Draining low-lying marshy land on the coast and using it for farming, etc.

Reformation Religious revolution in the sixteenth century, when Protestant religions broke away from the Roman Catholic Church.

Renaissance The rebirth of interest in the ancient Greek and Roman civilizations during the fifteenth and sixteenth centuries.

salons Entertainments or parties given by rich people, especially in Paris.

samurai A Japanese warrior.

Second Estate The clergy, especially in France.

serfs People who had to work in one place for one person and were not allowed to move away. If their local lord sold the land, they were sold to the new owner as well.

shoguns Powerful army leaders in Japan, who controlled the emperor and the country from the twelfth century until 1868.

spectrum The range of colors produced by splitting white light with a prism.

Spinning Jenny A machine for spinning cotton, invented by James Hargreaves in 1764.

Sun King A name for Louis XIV of France.

tapu A New Zealand word meaning "forbidden," from which we get "taboo."

Third Estate The ordinary people, mostly middle class, especially of France.

Vikings People from Scandinavia who made many voyages and war-raids on other European countries from the eighth to the tenth centuries.

water-frame A machine for spinning cotton, run by water power, invented by Richard Arkwright in 1769.

witchetty grub An edible Australian grub.

INDEX

Further Reading

GENERAL

The Times Atlas of World History ed. by George Barraclough (Hammond, 1989)

World History for Children and Young Adults by Vandelia VanMeter (Libraries Unlimited, 1992)

World History: a Brief Introduction by Joseph Reither (McGraw-Hill, 1973)

The Penguin Atlas of North American History to 1870 by Colin McEvedy (Viking Penguin, 1988)

War and Weapons by Brian Williams (Random House, 1987)

Farm Through the Ages by Philip Steele (Troll, 1992)

EUROPE

Seventeenth Century Interior Decoration in England by Peter Thornton (Yale, 1978)

Versailles by Gerald Van Der Kemp (Outlet, 1988)

The Eighteenth Century by Ruby Jennifer (Trafalgar Square, 1989)

THE REST OF THE WORLD

Cultural Atlas of China by Caroline Blunden (Facts On File, 1983)

China: A Concise Cultural History by Arthur Cotterell (NAL/Dutton, 1990)

History of Africa by K. Shillington (Macmillan, 1989)

First Americans: Forbidden Land by William Sarabande (Bantam, 1989)

The First Americans: Tribes of North America by Jane W. Watson (Pantheon, 1980)

Everyday Life in Early America by David F. Hawke (HarperCollins, 1989)

Picture Acknowledgements

The author and publishers would like to acknowledge, with thanks, the following photographic sources:

p. 10 Mansell Collection; p. 11. Ancient Art & Architecture Collection; p. 12 Mansell Collection; p. 13 Bridgeman Art Library, p. 15 (left) Institute of Agricultural History & Museum of English Rural Life; p. 15 (right) Mansell Collection; p. 17 Walker Art Gallery; p. 18 Bridgeman Art Library; p. 19 Ancient Art & Architecture Collection; p. 21 Michael Holford; p. 23 (upper & lower) AKG, p. 23 (right) Reunion des Musees Nationaux; p. 24 Michael Holford; p. 25 By Gracious Permission of Her Majesty the Queen; p. 26 Sonia Halliday Photographs; p. 27 AKG; p. 28 AKG; p. 29 (left) Ancient Art & Architecture Collection, p. 29 (right) AKG; p. 30 Giraudon; p. 31 (upper, centre, upper right & lower left) AKG; p. 31 (lower centre & right) Mary Evans Picture Library; p. 33 (left) Mary Evans Picture Library, p. 33 (right) National Maritime Museum; p. 34 Bridgeman Art Library; p. 37 (left) Michael Holford, p. 37 (right) Robert Harding Picture Library; p. 39 (left) Michael Holford, p. 39 (right) Bridgeman Art Library; p. 43 Robert Harding Picture Library (below) AKG; p. 45 Peter Newark's Western Americana; p. 46 AKG; p. 47 (upper) Peter Newark's American Pictures, p. 47 (lower) Mansell Collection; p. 48 AKG; p. 49 (upper left) Ancient Art & Architecture Collection, p. 49 (upper & lower right) Bridgeman Art Library, p. 49 (lower left) Mansell Collection; p. 50 AKG; p. 51 AKG; p. 52 AKG; p. 53 (upper) Bulloz, p. 53 (lower) Giraudon; p. 57 Scala; p. 58 Michael Holford; p. 59 (upper) British Library; p. 59 (lower) Rijksmuseum Foundation; p. 60 (upper) National Portrait Gallery; p. 60 (lower) British Library; p. 61 British Library; p. 63 Werner Forman Archive; p. 64 Mansell Collection; p. 66 AKG; p. 67 (upper & centre) Toula Antonakos; p. 67 (right) Robert Harding Picture Library; p. 68 Aukland City Art Gallery; p. 69 (left) Michael Holford, p. 69 (right) Aukland City Art Gallery; p. 70 Hulton-Deutsch Collection; p. 71 Werner Forman Archive. Wherever possible the copyright holder has been notified but we apologize if any material appears in error.